Your Journey With Jesus

Get Ready to Change Your Life this Year

Ron Nikkel

CHRISTIAN FOCUS

Ron Nikkel is the President of Prison Fellowship International, a global organisation of national Prison Fellowship organizations in 112 countries whose mission is to mobilise and assist the Christian Community in its ministry to prisoners, ex-prisoners, victims and their families. He travels extensively and has visited more than 600 prisons in 100 countries.

He is a Canadian and resides in Cape Breton Island, Nova Scotia with his wife Celeste and their two border collies.

Unless otherwise noted all Scripture quotations from the NIV (Holy Bible New International Version, Copyright © 1973, 1978, 1984 by the International Bible Society, Zondervan Bible Publishers).

Copyright © Ron Nikkel

ISBN 1-84550-152-7
ISBN 978-1-84550-152-5

10 9 8 7 6 5 4 3 2 1

Published in 2006
by
Christian Focus Publications,
Geanies House, Fearn, Tain,
Ross-shire, IV20 1TW, Scotland

www.christianfocus.com

Cover design by Danie Van Straaten

Printed and bound by Nørhaven Paperback A/S

Contents

PREFACE

YOU CAN'T GET THERE FROM HERE!

I have come to realize that knowing God is not the same as knowing about God: Believing the facts about the birth, life, death, and resurrection of Jesus Christ is no substitute for a personal relationship with Jesus Christ.

While I know a great deal about some people -- the intimate secrets and the hidden details of their lives, their psychological and physical profiles, I don't really know them personally because we had not lived, worked, or done anything together. It is only through passing time together in shared experiences, thoughts and dreams, failures and success, challenges and conflicts that I came to know a few people in a personal way. Genuine friendship develops in the process of sharing my life with another person; friendship is not realized just by studying and learning things about that person. My friendships have grown out of shared experiences, and in the journey of two lives coming together. I have never been able to seize friendship simply through study, desire, or even declarations of friendship.

A few years ago my wife, Celeste, and I were on a road trip through the majestic Rocky Mountains. Expecting to reach our destination by way of a scenic mountain pass, I had taken a winding road that seemed to be leading in the right direction. I knew we weren't lost, but I was becoming increasingly frustrated. After traveling for several hours we found ourselves driving down a narrow road along a never-ending river. The scenery was spectacular but as the paved road gave way to gravel which in turn gave way to a rugged logging track, we began wondering if we might have taken a wrong turn somewhere.

Like many "self-sufficient" in-charge men I was not about to stop and ask anyone for directions. "Real men don't need directions," I told my wife only half jokingly. "I'll figure it out, besides which, we can't be very far off course." But as the road became less traveled I finally relented and stopped at a small gray weather-beaten roadside station to ask for help. As I explained our situation to the grizzled old tobacco-chewing man behind the counter, he looked at me quizzically shaking his head. "*Ya cain't exactly get thar from here,*" he drawled, "*you're gonna hafta turn back ta whar ya come from and follow them signposts til ya git thar.*"

I often think about the old man's words in relation to my spiritual life, my journey toward God. For as long as I can remember the destination has been clear, the goal of knowing and walking with God. I've studied the map of scripture and I've listened to the experiences of spiritual men and women; I've been trained in the church and I've learned the intricacies of theology and doctrine. But for the most part, except for prayer, Bible study, and church attendance I couldn't say that God and I had spent much time together. I was following a road toward knowing more about God rather than traveling with God and getting to know Him in the course the journey. It took me a quite some time along a winding road to realize that I couldn't get there "from where I was", I could not find friendship with God by continuing down the road I was traveling on.

I had to turn around to see the signposts, and as I did I realized that friendship with God is not a destination but that it is a relationship, a deepening friendship on a journey with Jesus who once said "I am the way to the Father...if you really know me you will know my Father as well." Slowly I began to understand what it means to journey with Jesus, and I began seeing signposts in my daily life that were indications and expressions of his presence along the way.

The journey with Jesus is as compelling and exciting a journey as I could ever have imagined to any destination. Yet none of us can get there from where we are until we turn to see the signposts of God's presence. The reflections on following pages will hopefully give you a glimpse into that journey and enable you to see the "signposts" of God's presence in the midst of everyday life – not just mine, but yours as well.

May you journey well.

1

A TAPESTRY OF GRACE

I was walking in the woods as snowflakes began drifting lightly from the pale gray winter sky. My slow stroll through the woodland smell of decaying autumn leaves and the gurgling sounds of a gentle creek was gradually transformed into a magical stroll through white iridescent paradise.

It seemed only fitting on this first day of a new year that the first snowfall of the season would arrive to grace the start of another year. Softly falling flakes floated slowly from the sky. Before my eyes the gray-brown autumnal landscape became transfigured into a carpet of jeweled white and pine trees clothed in fluffy gowns of snow. All was quiet, save the whisper of the flakes, and I dared to tread the hallowed ground of a heavenly masterpiece.

Amid the indescribable beauty of the moment I paused to look around and was amazed to see my footprints slowly disappearing. In no time they were gone, lost forever beneath virgin flakes of white. Not a trace of my steps remained. Around me lay the unspoiled majesty of a divine tapestry in which past and future were woven into a singularly beautiful harmony. Last year's decomposing leaves and next year's budding foliage wore the same pure coat of white.

Often I've wished that my life could be transformed as easily as this: that my errant wandering tracks through life could be covered and lost beneath some gentle grace of time. It was New Year's Day and as I looked back upon the path I'd walked during the past year I became only too aware of footprints I'd left behind that I wished would disappear without a trace. I wished that the prints of sarcastic criticism and anger, of selfish manipulation and deception, of lust and greed, and of willfulness and of distraction could also be lost underneath the clean white snow. What a distorted, tangled trail I tend to leave behind!

Standing all alone on the doorstep of the New Year I watched my footprints disappear beneath an undisturbed tapestry of intricately woven flakes. My past, my footprints were gone, and in their place this tapestry of beauty and grace had fallen from above. God Himself was covering my footprints with mercy and forgiveness as white as the snow around me.

A profound sense of gratitude and joy filled my heart as huge flakes of white danced from Heaven, as though each flake was choreographed by God Himself. 'This is grace,' I said out loud. What neither human effort nor passing years can cover, God's grace does. For like the falling snow, God's grace falls down from Heaven upon my errant paths, and embraced by His love I know I am forgiven.

God's grace is complete and final, making it possible for us to leave the past behind and move forward with confidence. The footprints we've left behind have left their mark but are now unseen forever beneath God's tapestry of grace.

'Come now, let us reason together,' says the LORD.
'Though your sins are like scarlet,
    they shall be as white as snow;
though they are red as crimson,
    they shall be like wool' (Isa. 1:18).

2

CHRONICLES OF TIME

Sometimes I wonder if I am missing out on something. I feel like there is a possibility that life is passing me by. I scarcely have time to see and experience all the things I've dreamed and do all the things I've wanted. Feelings like this have become particularly acute for me in the wake of a neighbor's sudden death and two friends who have become seriously ill. The past few years have whizzed right by me. I've no sooner crossed the threshold into another year than I find myself well into it. Time does not stand still!

Few people have lived as interesting and rich a life as the late Malcolm Muggeridge. Before rising to the world stage as a celebrated British journalist and broadcaster, Muggeridge served as a teacher and journalist in Egypt and India, as a spy in Mozambique during World War II, and as a news correspondent in Washington, Moscow and Manchester. As a young man of caustic wit, incisive intellect and insightful perception, he approached life with incredible zest and insatiable curiosity. He always sought the widest and deepest experiences that life had to offer. His writings reflect a zest for life and relationships as well as an uncanny insight into the realities behind the façade of social customs and institutions.

Ever the skeptic and social critic, it was not until he reached middle age that Muggeridge personally began wrestling with the deeper questions related to the purpose of his own life. Ultimately he came to embrace a profound faith in Jesus Christ. Years later in his autobiography he described much of his life as a 'Chronicle of Wasted Time,' the story of a man so captivated by the sound, fury, and variety of human experience that he scarcely heard the still, small voice of divine purpose. Yet ultimately life experience became more than just a series of interesting destinations and encounters for him; it became the staging ground for eternity, for faith.

In reading Muggeridge's autobiography I realize again that my own time is not a commodity to be used like a renewable resource, or conserved like a budget, or focused on activity and accomplishment in pursuit of success and significance. Time is a priceless gift. I cannot undo or redo the time that is behind me, for it is gone. Nor can I seize the time yet to come, for it may not be mine to seize. The only time I actually have is the present moment of this day.

There are perspectives from which we can view the time given to us. The first is 'kronos' and the second is 'kairos.' *Kronos* is time seen and experienced simply as the measurable streaming of one moment, day, or year into another – one-thing-after-another time. It is the continuing flow of minutes, hours, days, weeks, months, and years that we scarcely think about. As we age, time becomes more and more precious for many of us, while for others it becomes increasingly burdensome. *Kronos* or chronological time is often experienced as the pressure of having too much to do and not enough time, or an interminable emptiness of waiting, yearning, and remembering.

Kairos time is different from *kronos*. It is the power and potential of the present moment. It is the 'now' experienced as being pregnant with meaning, significance, and opportunity. It is the holy value and importance of the moment that we are conscious of when we say that the time is right, or that we are on the threshold of a new era, or that a coincidence is perfectly timed. In the context of faith, *kairos* is the presence of the divine in each moment of time – God is present to us, around us, and in us, giving this moment divine and eternal significance. All of time, each single moment, is a holy gift for a holy purpose.

Like Malcolm Muggeridge, I've experienced far too much of my life as the mere chronology of interesting experiences and routine activities – much of it wasted in pursuit of selfish endeavors. At the beginning of this New Year I am acutely conscious of the progression of time, and the reality that my time will eventually run out. But I have become increasingly conscious that this moment, this day, is a holy gift. It is a *kairos* moment, a *kairos* day in which God is present, acting in and through me.

There is a time for everything,
   and a season for every activity under heaven:
      a time to be born and a time to die,
      a time to plant and a time to uproot ...
      a time to weep and a time to laugh
      a time to mourn and a time to dance...
      a time to be silent and a time to speak....

I have seen the burden God has laid on men. He has made everything beautiful in its time. He has also set eternity in the hearts of men; yet they cannot fathom what God has done from beginning to end... I know that everything God does will endure forever; nothing can be added to it and nothing taken from it. God does it so that men will revere him (Eccles. 3:1-2, 4, 7, 10-11, 14).

3

'DRY BONES'

I've been experiencing a time of feeling spiritually shriveled. I feel dried up like the sun-scorched clay of a riverbed where waters have ceased to run. My soul resonates with David who wrote a Psalm about his bones creaking and groaning within him all day long.

I have just come through a time of extraordinary spiritual encouragement, of worship, learning, and fellowship. I have even been involved in ministry, reaching out to needy people. How can it be that I suddenly find myself feeling like I am in a spiritual desert, a wasteland? Why has God forsaken me?

At first I thought I might just be exhausted, coming down from a spiritual high and from giving out to other people. Perhaps that was part of it because real ministry and giving can only proceed from what one has, not from a spiritual resource one doesn't have. It makes some sense, then, that the reservoir from which I have been giving has been emptied and needs to be renewed and replenished.

But the dry barrenness I feel seems to be more complicated than just refilling the spiritual cup from which I have given to others. The anguish of my heart is like that of a man crawling across the burning expanse of desert sand toward a lush, green, spring-fed oasis in the distance. Without a drink from that cool, clear spring, he will parch and perish. The problem is that, like him, I don't feel like I have the energy or strength to reach that oasis.

I know I'm spiritually parched, so I arise early in the morning to pray. But soon my mind wanders and I fall back asleep. I awake and turn to the Word, but somehow I just can't find anything that really connects with where I'm at. In pain my heart cries out to God, 'Help me Lord for I cannot help myself, my soul is parched with thirst and I have not the strength to drink.' In the silence that follows I long and wait for Him to draw me to the living water.

This has not been my first experience with spiritual dryness. It has happened often enough during the course of my busy life. When I'm busy and productive and engaged with other people, I feel good about myself and almost inadvertently begin to see myself as bigger than life – almost as a 'savior' kind of guy. It feels good to reach out and help other people. But now it seems that in the midst of all the helping I've been doing, God is reminding me that I, too, need help and cannot help myself.

Spiritual dryness is like physical thirst. A thirsty man needs water, and one who is spiritually dry needs to drink deeply from the fountain of God's renewing grace. Spiritual dryness is the experience of being a parched man in parched land with no ability to quench his own thirst. Could it be that this 'dry bones' feeling I have is God's reminder of how dependent I am on Him? Just when I'm feeling great about being a blessing to others He reminds me that I need constantly to drink from the spring of living water. This feeling of spiritual dryness and thirst is the tug of God on my soul that cannot quench its own thirst. It is a gift!

Only thirsty people seek water and recognize how dependent they really are.

As the deer pants for streams of water,
    so my soul pants for you, O God.
My soul thirsts for God, for the living God...
Deep calls to deep
    in the roar of your waterfalls;
all your waves and breakers
    have swept over me.
By day the LORD directs his love,
    at night his song is with me –
    a prayer to the God of my life (Ps. 42:1-2, 7-8).

4

THE CROSS IS NOT ENOUGH

'The cross is not enough,' he stated rather bluntly as we walked across the compound of the massive Russian prison. I was somewhat shocked by this sudden pronouncement by the burly prison director. After all, we had just visited the newly completed prison chapel with its magnificent iconostasis and gilded cross. I thought the chapel was a profound statement and symbol of the triumph of the cross over atheistic socialism; it represented the only real hope for the prisoners. My heart had surged with joy and gratitude as we entered the holy silence of the chapel and knelt to pray for the salvation of prisoners and comfort for their families.

Now as we returned across the compound toward the administration block I stopped to look back at the chapel. 'What do you mean when you say the cross is not enough?' I asked. 'Yes, the cross is now in prison,' he replied almost belligerently. 'Most of the prisoners even wear crosses around their necks, but it is not enough to change their way of life. I don't see a difference.' We continued our discussion. While it was obvious that the director was not a believer, I could not dismiss his statement as simply being the cynicism of an unrepentant former Communist.

Somewhat reluctantly, I conceded that he was right. For the symbol of the cross really is not enough. As powerful, meaningful, and holy an icon as it is, if it were not for the holy reality behind the symbol, the cross would be nothing more than a thing, an artifact. Apart from the historical truth of Jesus, God crucified, dead, and resurrected, the cross is simply an ancient artifact of human torture.

Some years earlier a priest told me the story of his ministry helping men coming out of prison by providing them with emergency shelter, clothing, and food in the name of Jesus. On one occasion a burly ex-prisoner angrily confronted him by tearing open the front of his shirt to reveal a neck-to-navel crucifix tattoo. 'I have all the religion I need,' he shouted. 'I don't need your preaching.' Quietly and slowly the priest replied, 'Yes, I can see you have the cross on your chest, but is it in your heart?'

The reality is that the power of the cross is not in the symbol, not in the artifact, but in Jesus. In fact there have probably been thousands upon thousands of crosses through history on which criminals, terrorists, and traitors have been brutally executed. However, it is not because of the thousands who have been crucified that the cross has been imbued with lasting significance. It is only because of the 'One,' Jesus the Christ. Apart from Jesus, the cross doesn't have any more significance than a hangman's noose, an electric chair, or a lethal injection, and it is not the mark of the cross but the indelible mark of Jesus on a human life that makes the difference.

Although I found myself agreeing with the prison director's assertion that the cross is not enough, I was cringing inwardly because the cross is more than merely an artifact of culture, fashion, or religious identification. For me it is the profoundly sacred icon of God's redemptive mercy and transforming power. As such, it stands at the very crux of my faith. Yet I cringed because the stinging indictment of his observation was partly true. For when the cross is reduced to a symbol divorced from its true meaning, it becomes useless. The gilded cross above the prison chapel would never be enough to transform that prison apart from the presence of the church and its proclamation of truth, and its witness to the depth of God's love. The cross around an inmate's neck has no power to transform him, apart from his personal faith and repentance at the bloodstained feet of the One who hung on the cross as Savior of the universe.

The cross is not enough! The crosses with which we adorn ourselves often seem to be nothing more than fashion accessories – artifacts. The crosses on church steeples and altars are so ordinary that we tend not to think about their real significance, and see them as merely accoutrements of our religious architecture and décor. Making the sign of the cross so easily becomes a reflex action devoid of Godward consciousness.

I wonder what would happen if the cross on every church really came to stand for the sacrificial love of the people in that church for their neighbors, their community, and the world? I wonder what would happen if the crosses we wear really came to represent the lifestyle of our faith in action. I wonder what would happen if making the sign of the cross was borne out in my own life as one 'crucified with Christ.' What does it mean to embrace the cross in all that it truly symbolizes?

A few days ago I came across a provocative little statement that I have not been able to get out of my mind: 'A crucified Messiah must have crucified followers.' Symbols are not enough!

Lord, you said that when you were exalted on the cross,
    You would draw all hearts to you.
By dying on the cross for us, you have already drawn to your love
    So many who, for your sake, have forsaken all things –
    their goods, their country, their relatives, and their life.
Draw also my poor heart, which, through your grace, now pants to love you.
O death of Jesus, O love of Jesus,
    Take possession of all my thoughts and affections,
    And grant that, for the future, to please you, O Jesus,

May be the sole object of all my thoughts and desires.
O most amiable Lord, hear my prayer,
    through the merits of your death. Amen[1]

---

[1] St Alphonsus Liguori, 'Prayer to Jesus on the Cross.' Quoted in Heart to Heart, Praying With the Saints, Word Among Us Press, 2000.

5

IN THE FACE OF EVIL

I was in Rwanda and had come face to face with the work of the Devil – depravity and evil of unimaginable horror and proportion. It was an excruciating spiritual and emotional experience, and I was angry. I cannot begin describing the gruesome, putrid stench of the thousands of corpses that remained in open view at genocide sites around the country. Men, women, children, and infants, club-bludgeoned and machete-slashed to death by ordinary people trained to hate and mobilized to massacre their neighbors as the 'final solution' in cleansing the bloodline of the nation.

Anesthetized by the comfort of my way of life, I had been led to believe that this was just another African intertribal conflict of little greater consequence. The horrific specter of blatant genocide had been downplayed by international political leaders, complicit in the horror by their lack of courage to intervene. So they averted their eyes and ours from the perpetrators and turned deaf ears to the screams of victims and survivors. In fewer than a hundred days, nearly one million Rwandan Tutsis and moderate Hutus were systematically executed by Hutu extremists in one of the fastest and most vicious acts of genocide in recorded human history. With wanton hatred, the perpetrators incited the unrestrained slaughter of innocent people.

Some of the survivors took me to places of unthinkable carnage and destruction – scenes that I wish I could forget, but will always remember. I could feel the unheeded cries of terror that were frozen on the faces of mothers, whose rotting arms were locked around the remains of their cowering children. With their rigormortic hands still raised in self-defense, the skull-crushed corpses of men were still postured helplessly where they had been brutally murdered. The macabre skeletal remnants of tens of thousands of victims were still inside the blood-soaked schools and churches where they had sought refuge only to find betrayal, often at the hands of their spiritual 'shepherds.' Tens of thousands of other corpses lay buried in mass graves and shallow latrines across the country, while the bodies of thousands who had been massacred in the streets were thrown into the lakes and rivers and lie buried without names, in hundreds of memorial gravesites.

As I tried to comprehend the enormity of this evil I felt as if I was struggling against the very force of evil. Although I had encountered the face of evil in the depravity of individual men and women I've met in prisons around the world, never had I encountered so closely the contorted face of evil on such a massive scale. After the war more than 130,000 genocide perpetrators and participants were imprisoned. Painfully, several victims told me that hundreds more continue living in the community as if nothing happened. Among those imprisoned are dozens of priests and pastors of many denominations who actively supported the killing of their own people. For me, one of the most painful realizations was the fact that Rwanda had long been known as one of the most Christianized countries in Africa. At one time more than eighty-six per cent of the country's inhabitants identified themselves as being Christian. It was a country in which the countryside, towns, and villages were abounding with churches.

'How is it possible that such horrible evil could take root and flourish in a Christian country?' I wondered. 'And what now? How will the Christian message of forgiveness and reconciliation and justice be heard? How can it make a difference in the face of evil?'

I was conscious that I was only an outsider looking in and that it was impossible for me to fully comprehend the depth of Rwanda's experience. Yet in listening to the horror stories of the people, visiting the blood-soaked genocide sites, smelling the putrid fear of decaying corpses, and feeling echoes of their terrible screams, I was gripped by anger and rage against the injustice and evil. I cried to God for judgment and vengeance against those who raped, pillaged, and butchered their neighbors, who scorned their pleas for mercy, who snuffed out their children's lives and who desecrated the sanctuaries of their faith. What kind of justice can ever address such genocidal evil?

As a follower of Jesus Christ I know that violent justice only perpetuates violence and will not break the cycle of evil. Only grace and forgiveness can accomplish that. At the same time justice demands that evil be unmasked for what it is and that the truth of complicity in evil be revealed, that perpetrators be accountable for their actions. The only hope I saw in Rwanda was when I met with Tutsi victims and survivors who felt bound to forgive those who butchered their family members and friends. It was the only way they could release themselves from dreadful captivity to anger and the thirst for revenge. I met with Hutu killers who participated in the genocide, men who dared to own up to their involvement. It was the only way for them to find release from the unbearable nightmares of their own guilt.

The Bible speaks of overcoming evil with good. In Rwanda I realized that good is not a matter of ignoring evil, but that it involves humility to tell the truth; courage to turn aside from retaliation and revenge; love to reach out and to embrace enemies, and faith in God's own power to forgive, to heal; and to restore. I wonder if the genocide would have ever happened if the church and followers of Jesus had learned how to live this way before.

27

You have heard that it was said, 'Love your neighbour and hate your enemy.' But I tell you: Love your enemies and pray for those who persecute you, that you may be sons of your Father in heaven. He causes his sun to rise on the evil and the good, and sends rain on the righteous and the unrighteous. If you love those who love you, what reward will you get? (Matt. 5:43-46).

6

WHEN JUSTICE AND MERCY MEET

'Please, Your Honor, have mercy on me,' pled one of the accused defendants as he faced the judge to hear his sentence.

'Please, Lord, have mercy on me,' I prayed as I contemplated my sins.

The defendant before the judge was a notorious repeat offender who had no redeeming qualities, no positive reasons to be spared from the harshest penalty of the law. Kneeling before the Lord, I likewise realized that I am a notorious repeat offender and that I can offer no legitimate defense as to why I have committed the same sin for the umpteenth time. Yet I am confident that, while the judge will probably not be lenient with the defendant, God will have mercy on me.

As a Christian, I have a well-developed understanding of right and wrong, and a conscience shaped to know when I am guilty of wrongdoing. Nearly every day I end up facing the Lord to ask for His forgiveness and mercy in response to my sin and guilt. I know my guilt and that I am without excuse. I have nothing to present except myself as a poor beggar desperately in need of mercy.

Strangely though, the mercy I desire and am so quick to seek is a mercy I am slow to give. I understand the judge who spurns the defendant's plea for mercy because there is nothing in the defendant's record or behavior to warrant any reconsideration of the sentence. All too often that is how I react to people who are guilty of offending or insulting me. I become their accuser and their judge. My judgment is often quick and complete – instantaneous!

How is it that the joyful release and freedom I experience when God has mercy on me is of so little relevance when I demand justice for my offenders and detractors? How can I possibly be the one who prays to the Lord, 'Forgive us our trespasses as we forgive those who trespass against us?' Am I alone in this?

If the degree of our mercy toward others was indeed the degree of God's mercy toward any of us, Heaven would be a desolate place indeed. I wonder how the mercy we desire and the justice we demand have become such polar opposites? During the time of the prophet Micah, those who believed in God were as devout and faithful to the church as most of us. They tried hard to keep the commandments and were involved in all kinds of religious duties and activities. But in the process, they had forgotten God and the great love and mercy He had showered upon them; how He had freed them from the tyranny of slavery; how He had repeatedly rescued them from enemy armies; how He had provided for them in times of great need. Their religious beliefs had become divorced from the realities and complexities of day-to-day living to the point that they showed little mercy or compassion to the widows, orphans, strangers, and offenders in their own communities. These people, who owed their very existence to God's mercy, had become unmerciful and arrogant.

One of the greatest literary parables of God's grace and man's struggle between justice and mercy is Victor Hugo's *Les Misérables*. The main character, Jean Valjean, has spent nineteen years in prison for stealing a loaf of bread and upon his release from prison he is required to wear a 'parole ticket.' Like many ex-prisoners he finds himself shunned by society and resorts to thievery in order to survive. Finally Valjean rips the parole ticket from his jacket and attempts to begin a new life.

For nearly twenty years, however, he is pursued by Inspector Javert, a tenacious police detective who refuses to let Valjean go unpunished. In a climactic twist of fate, student revolutionaries capture Inspector Javert, bind him, and turn him over to Valjean for revenge. Valjean takes Inspector Javert to an empty street where he orders him to turn around. Javert complies, fully expecting that the man he has pursued for so many years will shoot him. But to his utter astonishment, Valjean cuts the Inspector loose and sends him on his way. Valjean's show of mercy toward him becomes more than the Inspector can bear. Confused and angry, he drowns himself in the River Thames.

Valjean had been forgiven much, blessed much, and redeemed much, while Javert had become so obsessed with justice that he became blind to mercy. Mercy seems to make no sense when justice is required. We tend to experience and think of justice and mercy as polar opposites. And yet our merciful Lord calls us through Micah to walk with humility before Him, evidenced in doing justice and loving mercy. According to the law, Valjean should have been returned to prison for violating his parole. But God spared Valjean, and he later proved his total transformation by sparing his arch-pursuer, Javert.

Justice and mercy are not polar opposites; they are vitally interconnected. To separate one from the other renders both meaningless and empty. Were it not for mercy, every human being would live and die with the inescapable consequence of guilt. No reprieve, no forgiveness, no way out. Echoing the words of St Augustine, Cardinal Jaime Sin of Manila observed that, 'Justice without mercy is tyranny. Mercy without justice is weakness. When justice and mercy meet, there is the grace of God.'

He has showed you, O man, what is good.
    And what does the LORD require of you?
To act justly and to love mercy
    and to walk humbly with your God (Micah 6:8).

7

OVERCOMING EVIL

As much as I desire mercy in the face of my misdeeds, I also want to live in a society where justice is done. But I struggle with the idea that justice is accomplished by locking someone up in prison for punishment and then expecting that this will somehow result in the betterment of a person who has done evil. But how else can we possibly overcome evil in our communities and the world?

Over the years I have had the opportunity of meeting thousands of prisoners and hundreds of criminal justice officials throughout the world. My travels have taken me to the best of prisons and the worst of prisons: from gleaming modern facilities that irate law-and-order advocates call 'four star hotels,' to stinking underground dungeons that others call 'hell on earth.' I know many prisoners who have suffered horrible deprivation and cruelty in the hands of the criminal justice system, but I have also met prisoners who enjoy greater comfort in prison than they ever experienced on the outside.

Yet regardless of the conditions of confinement or the adaptation of prison inmates to institutional life, prison does not make 'bad' men 'good,' because prison does not overcome or erase the evil that lies within the human heart. It is one of the great myths of society that simply locking up more offenders and 'throwing away the keys' will help to win the fight against crime. One only has to visit a court of criminal law or a prison to know that prisons are like revolving doors, recycling offenders again and again.

Judges are all too familiar with the fact that the offenders they sentence to prison will eventually return to the streets, probably in worse shape than when they were sent to prison. Prisons are literally infectious moral cesspools that incubate human immorality and evil. The dominant influence in prison is the influence of men and women who are confined because of their illegal behavior.

As necessary as prisons may be to keep offenders out of public circulation for periods of time, prisons do not offer a cure for evil. Released prisoners seldom return to the community as morally better persons upon completion of their sentence.

Prisons have taught me that punishment is not enough to achieve justice and that evil is not overcome through judgment and punishment. But, in a way I have never known before, in the midst of prison I have come face to face with the power of 'good' overcoming evil – the transforming power of a compassionate, loving Heavenly Father. Amid the futility of imprisonment I have seen evidence of the Good Shepherd rescuing fallen and lost men and women from the clutches of sin and evil. I have seen the Loving Father embrace unloved and unloving offenders with arms of forgiveness and acceptance. I have seen the God of justice extend mercy and hope to hardcore criminals. I have seen the ugliness and stench of unimaginable human depravity beautifully transformed by the power of the Creator. I have seen goodness overcoming evil through forgiveness as relationships between victims and offenders are reconciled and restored.

It is only grace and mercy that sets prisoners free from the downward spiral of evil. Only the light of truth overcomes the darkness of moral corruption. For me, prisons are a cogent demonstration that social retribution, community rejection, judicial sanctions, imposed discipline, and severe punishment can never ultimately vanquish evil. While prisons may be necessary, they are not the solution to crime and evil. Evil can only be overcome with good – the redemptive love and transforming power of Jesus Christ.

At least, that's my experience...

You see, at just the right time, when we were still powerless, Christ died for the ungodly. Very rarely will anyone die for a righteous man, though for a good man someone might possibly dare to die. But God demonstrates his own love for us in this: While we were still sinners, Christ died for us (Rom. 5:6-8).

8

DIFFICULTIES OF THE OTHER CHEEK

Whether I've been hurt by a personal slight or insult or victimized by some other offense committed against me, my reaction is to fight back.

I was traveling through an east African country during a period of rising crime and lawlessness. Shopkeepers and ordinary citizens of the capital city were growing increasingly outraged and intolerant as street criminals brazenly ruled the streets in broad daylight. Finally they'd had enough; even the police seemed unable to curb the tide of crime. Frustration and anger had reached the boiling point when yet another offender was caught in the act of breaking into a parked car in front of a shop. The shopkeeper, joined by a growing crowd of people, chased the offender down the street. What happened when they caught him was detailed in the newspapers the next day as another incident of mob justice. It was a 'necklacing' – the captured man was bound and then a rubber tire soaked in gasoline was put around his neck and set ablaze to teach him and others a lesson. While the actual details of the incident were gruesome, the satisfaction of the people was evident. 'Justice had been done – served him right,' they said.

Now, I will admit that when I read the article it was not without an instinctive nod of approval. The good guys won; it was a victory over crime and a lesson taught to other street thieves! Of course my sensibility quickly took over. With a feeling of moral superiority I characterized the incident as being a bloodthirsty and vengeful overreaction. After all, the man had only attempted to break into a parked car. He shouldn't have had to pay for it with his life.

What if it had been my car and I had been the one to catch him in the act? Would I have joined the chase? Or what if my wife and I had been walking down the street when suddenly a thief came from behind and snatched the handbag from her arm? Would I have caught him and delivered justice of my own?

Jesus said, 'You have heard that it was said, "Eye for eye, and tooth for tooth." But I tell you, Do not resist an evil person. If someone strikes you on the right cheek, turn to him the other also.' These words totally contradict my natural instincts and sense of fair play. It just doesn't seem to make any sense to accept evil or encourage it by not fighting back.

For years these words from the Sermon on the Mount have troubled me. If no one resists evil, won't evil rule the day? Isn't evil ignored, evil encouraged? While reactions to evil like the 'necklacing' incident go too far, I understand the motivation toward vengeance and retaliation. No one wants to be a passive victim. And yet I realize that revenge inevitably goes beyond just exacting an 'eye for an eye,' and ends up escalating violence and evil. According to some biblical scholars, what Jesus was teaching was not passivity but a response to evil that would defuse the violence involved by neither mirroring nor magnifying the initial offense through violent retaliation.

Turning the other cheek is far more than a passive response to evil. It is a profound example of responding to a wrongful act by drawing attention to its evil. It is probably by no accident that St Matthew pointedly refers to the right cheek as being struck. In a world of predominantly right-handed people, it is not possible to be face to face with another person and to be struck on the right cheek except by way of a backhanded slap. In the cultural context of Jesus' time a backhanded slap (that is to strike someone with the back of one's hand) was an intentionally dismissive and derogatory act, often reflected in the relationship between a domineering, abusive master and a humiliated slave.

In response to such an abusive and demeaning violation of one's personhood, Jesus suggests neither retaliation nor passivity, but the courageous confrontation of the offender by turning the other cheek. Such a response is profoundly significant, for now the evil-doer is confronted with his own evil. The humiliated and offended person neither cowers in submission nor reacts in anger. Rather, with dignity, the victim turns around to present the other cheek. The tables have been turned. Indignity and violation meet with dignity and courage. The offender is confronted by the evil of his action and will either have to show himself for what he is, turn away, or engage as a person with the offended. He must either walk away recognizing the failure of his action, or draw further attention to his own inhumanity by adding injury to his insult. In either case, he cannot hide the evil of his deed behind the response of the injured. He is surprised, caught in the glaring spotlight of his own indecency.

In *Les Misérables*, the classic story by Victor Hugo referred to in a previous chapter, the desperate Jean Valjean finally found shelter and hospitality in the home of a bishop, but then proceeded to steal the silverware and escape into the night. The ill-fated thief was seized by the police who, upon finding the silverware in his possession, recognized it as being the bishop's. They dragged the hapless Valjean back to the bishop's residence in the middle of the night to prove the charges against him. Confronted by the police and Valjean, the bishop quietly and gently turned the other cheek. 'The silverware was a gift,' he said. Then picking up two silver candlesticks, he handed them to Valjean, reminding him that he had 'forgotten' to include them with the rest of the silverware. With the candlesticks and the rest of the silverware,

Valjean was sent on his way. In one powerful moment the cycle of evil and violence had been broken by an act that transcended the mentality of both the accusers and accused. The bishop turned the other cheek. In so doing he unmasked Valjean's thievery, exposing him to grace.

I don't know if it would be naive to respond to all personal encounters with crime and evil in this way or not. Yet in Jesus Christ I am confronted by my own evil most powerfully, not by His judgment and condemnation, but by the fact of His forgiveness and acceptance of me in the very face of my complicity and guilt. As a recipient of such incredible grace I cannot help but follow Jesus and to respond to my own offenders in a way that goes beyond 'tit for tat' and 'eye for eye' justice. To follow Jesus amid the everyday reality of insults, injuries, crime, and evil is to resist the instinctive tendency to do unto others as they *have done* unto me. It is to turn that tendency completely upside down by doing unto others as *Jesus has done unto me*. Knowing how to 'turn the other cheek' is not merely closing ones eyes to evil. It is responding to evildoers by transcending the violence and our own tendency to retaliate in like or greater measure. It is the courageous, powerful, and gracious confrontation of evil by a response that renders evil exposed for what it is, and that beckons the evil-doer into relationship – relationship with the offended and with Jesus Christ.

You have heard that it was said, 'Eye for eye, and tooth for tooth.' But I tell you, Do not resist an evil person. If someone strikes you on the right cheek, turn to him the other also. And if someone wants to sue you and take your tunic, let him have your cloak as well. If someone forces you to go one mile, go with him two miles (Matt. 5:38–41).

9

But for the Grace of God

I don't think there is any idea more radical and exciting than the grace of God.

One of my favorite stories is that of the captain of a slave ship during the 1750s. On an unusually stormy voyage to the West Indies, John Newton, captaining a British slave ship, came face to face with the wretched evil of slavery – the inhumanity and the awful degradation and suffering of the people he was transporting to be sold. For the first time, he recognized his personal complicity in evil and that he had no way of undoing what he had done. He was personally involved in and responsible for the misery of countless human beings that he was taking from Africa to the slave markets of the 'new world.' Through his realization of being irretrievably guilty, he came to embrace the good news of God's grace in Jesus Christ and turned his back on the slave trade. In a profound expression of his gratitude for God's grace, he wrote the enduring words of the well-known hymn, 'Amazing Grace.' Leaving the lucrative profits of slave trading behind, John Newton became a minister, boldly proclaiming the good news of God's grace and forgiveness for all offenders.

I heard someone remark that every saint has a history and that every sinner has a future. No one has a dark and inescapable past, and no one is beyond hope for the future. Who would have thought that John Newton could ever go from the lucrative exploitation of human beings, to being a passionate preacher of the gospel? Or who would have expected centuries earlier that a debauched and self-indulgent young African man named Augustine would become the Bishop of Hippo, one of the most influential and formative thinkers of the Christian church? Every saint, even each ordinary follower of Christ such as you and me, has an unsightly history. But thanks be to God that we are not outside the embrace of His grace.

Recently, as I was driving home from a day at the office, I saw a questionable-looking man standing by the side of the road hitch-hiking (begging for a ride). Impulsively I pulled over and offered him a ride. As he clambered unsteadily into the passenger seat, it was rather evident that he had been drinking, and all of a sudden I wanted him out of my clean car. My gut reaction was to write him off as a 'bum' and a loser. But, since I didn't have far to go I decided not to make an issue out of it and let him ride along.

During the next forty-five minutes he poured out a story of personal failure, pain, and futility. His wife had been diagnosed with schizophrenia and had recently been committed to a state psychiatric institution. Even prior to this he said that he had been chronically unemployed and wondered if his inability to provide for the family had somehow contributed to her problems. Following his wife's committal, their only child, a five-year-old daughter, had been removed from the home by child-welfare authorities and was being placed in foster care. And now his only sister had ordered him to move out of her house even though he had neither money, nor another place to stay, nor any work possibilities.

The hitch-hiker talked as if he had nothing to live for and no one who cared. As he spoke various thoughts went through my mind. I felt like asking him if he didn't think that a lot of the problems were his own fault – such as his drinking, his relationships, and his work ethic. I felt like telling him just to clean up his act and pull himself up by his own bootstraps. I had all kinds of advice that I wanted to give him. But something stopped me. It was just the simple thought, 'There but for the grace of God go I.'

I held back on giving him my free advice. As I dropped him off near his destination I simply bade him goodbye and, 'God bless you.' I turned toward my home feeling empty and wondering if I had ignored an opportunity to be more gracious than just giving the man a ride.

I know that God's grace extends beyond my limited ability to lend a helping hand to the hapless hitch-hiker or even offering him advice. I realized again that, just like him, I am totally dependent on God's grace. Amazing grace, indeed, that great men like John Newton and St Augustine are rescued from their sinful roots, and that hopeless, helpless men like the hitch-hiker are loved by the God who offers each of us a way forward.

Several years ago a college classmate of mine, who went on to become a respected professor of theology, became involved in an embarrassing intimate relationship outside of his marriage. In the process his wife left him and he was censured by the college and ultimately dismissed from his position. In the aftermath he faced continuing embarrassment, ridicule, and criticism from his colleagues, friends, and even family members. His children turned their backs on him. He had become a complete disgrace to those who had known and respected him. His life began falling apart as he found himself increasingly isolated and excluded.

Tragically, the community of faith, the very people who were themselves the beneficiaries and witnesses of God's amazing grace, pushed him away and rejected him. The professor had fallen from grace and there was no way back for him. What a tragedy it is when we presume to be the gatekeepers of God's grace by excluding people like the professor or the hitch-hiker, when they need it most. And how much poorer we all would be if the likes of a slave-trading John Newton or a self-indulgent St Augustine had been barred from grace!

But for the grace of God!

> For it is by grace you have been saved, through faith – and this not from yourselves, it is the gift of God – not by works, so that no one can boast. For we are God's workmanship, created in Christ Jesus to do good works, which God prepared in advance for us to do... [R]emember that at that time you were separate from Christ, excluded from citizenship ... foreigners to the covenants of the promise, without hope and without God in the world. But now in Christ Jesus you who once were far away have been brought near through the blood of Christ (Eph. 2:8-10, 12-13).

10

EMBARRASSMENT OR EMBRACE?

'Sir,' he said timidly, approaching me that blustery cold night. 'You wouldn't be able to help me out with $10 to buy some petrol, would you? We had to bring my mother-in-law to the hospital today and waited all day for her to be admitted. We have no money, and our three kids are alone at home.'

'What! Do I look gullible or something?' I thought, looking suspiciously at the man who was walking toward me across the hotel parking lot. I was not unaware that the hotel, with its pub and casino, was a popular gathering place for gamblers and for losers.

'See, my truck is right over there,' he continued, pointing to a dilapidated old truck at the far side of the parking lot. 'My wife and dog are inside. We haven't had anything to eat all day. We need to get home to our kids. Can you help me out?' he pleaded.

Now I don't mind admitting that I've fallen for stories like this before and I swore I'd never be an easy mark again. As he continued pouring out his tale of woe I thought that, as compelling as the story sounded, he had probably come into the city for a good time and had squandered away his last dollar – the needs of his wife and three kids notwithstanding. I was quite sure that any $10 contribution toward petrol would quickly find its way into the slot machines or pub. He was clearly a loser!

The wind was biting cold. I was shivering and anxious to move on as I considered the man before me and his story of a hospitalized mother-in-law, three kids at home, and the wife and dog in the dilapidated pickup truck. His pleas for help hung suspended like ice particles in the frigid winter air between us.

'I'll come back in a couple of minutes,' I said, trying to get out of the situation without bluntly turning my back on him. While it wasn't my intention to return right away, I was hoping that by the time I returned he would either have grown tired of waiting or obtained $10 from someone more gullible than I. So, turning away, I walked quickly across the icy lot into the hotel restaurant where my wife and aunt were waiting. No sooner had I stepped into the warmth of the restaurant than I felt compelled to return to the man in the parking lot. He had asked me for help with petrol; how could I possibly write him off as undeserving and at the same time lie to him about coming back?

Back in the parking lot, I saw that he was waiting for me. I wondered for a moment if he really expected me to come back or if he was really just that desperate. My excuse had been feeble, so either he knew I'd turn soft or he was simply hoping against desperate hope that I'd come back to help him out. 'Follow me,' I said. 'I need petrol, too. Meet me at the petrol station across the street.'

As he pulled into the station behind me, I could see his wife and dog through the snow and ice-encrusted windshield of his truck. 'Do you want to pump it?' he inquired hesitatingly. 'No, you go ahead, I'll pump my own,' I responded. With that, he put the petrol nozzle into his gas tank. As the pump started I could hear the meter clicking up the amount and wondered just how much petrol he'd actually take. A few minutes later he removed the nozzle from his truck and turned off the pump. 'Are you sure that's enough to get you home?' I asked. 'Yeah,' he responded. 'It is, and thank you very much. God bless you!' With that, he started the truck and drove slowly into the night.

As I finished fueling the tank of my car I wondered if I had been used, once again falling prey to the lies of another loser with a good story. Like most people I don't mind giving to worthy causes and helping innocent, deserving people who are overtaken by trouble or difficult circumstances. I have very little sympathy for people, however, who have the ability to help themselves but resort to manipulating others. I resent people who live as social parasites, feeding on the generosity of those who are compassionate.

I've been thinking about this experience and what it means for me to be a responsible follower of Jesus. Against my higher expectations, natural inclinations, and good judgment, I find myself being drawn to the image of Jesus who beckons me from amongst the undeserving poor, criminals, drug addicts, and abusers. In the midst of those who are considered scum of the earth – users, losers, boozers, and the like – I see Jesus's heart of love and compassion for the misfits and the rejects of the world. From amongst them I hear the whisper of His love and mercy – 'It is not the healthy who need a doctor, but the sick ... I have not come to call the righteous, but sinners' (Matt. 9:12, 13).

For me the most unnatural, difficult, and embarrassing act in the world is to embrace someone who doesn't deserve to be embraced – while knowing their terrible faults and filthy failures, to reach out and embrace them as though I really cared. I am becoming increasingly aware that the awesome good news of the gospel is that the love of Jesus Christ is not like mine. With no preconditions, no strings attached, and without any reservation, the embrace of Jesus includes undeserving, irresponsible, unkind, embarrassing, and irreverent people.

As I saw the dilapidated truck drive off into the night, a phrase that Jesus spoke rang in my mind, '... and you came to me.' Jesus said some other things, too. But I realize He didn't say anything about clothing only the naked who were refugees, or feeding only victims of famine, or visiting only prisoners of injustice, or giving a cup of cold water only in times of drought. He said nothing about conditions or our own embarrassment. What He did say was that, by embracing people in need with compassion and generosity, we are embracing Him.

Ten dollars worth of petrol isn't much to most people. But still I wonder if that was an irresponsible and embarrassing lack of good judgment, or if I was actually embracing Jesus.

Come, you who are blessed by my Father; take your inheritance, the kingdom prepared for you since the creation of the world. For I was hungry and you gave me something to eat, I was thirsty and you gave me something to drink, I was a stranger and you invited me in, I needed clothes and you clothed me, I was sick and you looked after me, I was in prison and you came to visit me.... I tell you the truth, whatever you did for one of the least of these brothers of mine, you did for me (Matt 25:34-36, 40).

11

UNNATURAL ACTS OF LOVE

It was surely the scandal of the century, the preacher marrying the likes of her. Surely he had not been unaware of her reputation with the men. But marry her he did and still the woman slept around. She became a monstrous embarrassment to him. What made it even more embarrassing was that she got herself pregnant by another man. Typically, people thought him the fool and nodded knowingly behind his back. 'It's true,' they said. 'You can take a woman like her off the streets; but you can't take the streets out of a woman like her.'

Even after the birth of her first child she didn't change, for she was promiscuous and unfaithful to the core. Their marriage was a façade, non-existent. Although the preacher was painfully disappointed and embarrassed, he was an honorable man who stayed the course. When she finally deserted him for yet another lover that should have been the end of the matter. But no! The preacher went after her and literally paid off her lover so he could have his wife back.

The scandal of her affairs was one thing. But the scandal of the preacher deliberately taking her back was completely off the charts. No self-respecting man of common sense would open himself up to being burned and humiliated again. It was an unnatural act of love. Furthermore, why on earth would a decent 'man of God' continue in a relationship with someone as low-down and sleazy as her?

If anyone were to have asked the preacher, 'Why?', his answer would have been, 'It is the will of God.'

A friend of mine, Philip Yancey, told me that the relationship between the preacher and the prostitute resembles God's relationship with His people in the Old Testament. The picture of God that emerges in the Old Testament is that of the 'jilted lover.' After everything that God does to demonstrate His love for His people, they turn their backs on him and fall for other gods. Again and again, God shows compassion toward His beloved people. But again and again, like 'she-camels in heat,' they give themselves to foreign gods.

In a very poignant and painful way, the preacher came to understand something of the feelings God had for His beloved people. Hosea knew that it was God's will for him to marry Gomer and to stick with her even when she embarrassed, humiliated, and rejected him. God's love is neither thwarted nor aborted by the infidelity of His people. God may be a jilted lover, but He will always be the lover. Hosea came to understand that his painful relationship with Gomer was akin to the pain of God in the relationship with His chosen people. Hosea's suffering love for Gomer symbolized God's suffering love for unfaithful Israel. God is a wounded lover – rejected by the people He had chosen, and blessed, and led, and protected, and forgiven again and again.

The story of Hosea is one of the most powerful parables of the God who is long-suffering in His love. The God whose love for an unfaithful, prostituting people ultimately culminates in His coming to live among them as the incarnate God: Jesus Christ touches lepers to make them well, makes the lame walk, restores sight to the blind, embraces noisy children, eats and drinks with sinners, and responds to the pleas of beggars – only to end up being humiliated, rejected, and unjustly executed on the cross.

In this, God became the twice-wounded lover: first wounded by the unfaithfulness of His beloved people, and then wounded by trading His life for theirs, even though they might again refuse His love and turn their backs.

I cannot fathom the quality of such love. It's humanly impossible. What God asked Hosea to do in relationship to Gomer goes totally against our sensibilities, against our better judgment, and against our notion of love itself. Loving someone who spurns your love, who desecrates and tramples upon the best you have to offer, is uncalled for and irresponsible. It is an unnatural act of love, but that is the unrelenting love of our Heavenly Father.

Such love by which I myself am loved in spite of my infidelities goes beyond words, beyond feelings, and beyond reciprocity. The One who loves me so immeasurably and completely desires not just my faithfulness, but also my participation in His love.

Love one another. As I have loved you, so you must love one another. By this all men will know that you are my disciples, if you love one another.

As the Father has loved me, so have I loved you. Now remain in my love. If you obey my commands, you will remain in my love, just as I have obeyed my Father's commands and remain in his love. I have told you this so that my joy may be in you and that your joy may be complete. My command is this: Love each other as I have loved you. Greater love has no one than this, that he lay down his life for his friends (John 13:34-35; 15:9-13).

12

LOVE IN THE RUINS

On a cold, dreary Sunday morning I went to a prison to participate in the chapel service. It was my first visit to that particular prison in Argentina and I discovered that the service was being held in a ward for the criminally insane. I overcame my initial feeling of disappointment because I had been looking forward to visiting the prison with a group of enthusiastic young people who had been visiting the prison quite regularly. It was a bit disconcerting, however, to find myself in a cramped, stuffy, smoke-filled medical ward filled with cots of men with blank stares, drooling mouths, and weird mannerisms. 'Why bother?' I thought to myself. 'It would make far more sense for the group to visit inmates in the general prison population. This was a total dead end!'

I stood to the side observing as the volunteers began circulating among the bedridden inmates. The gloom of the ward seemed to lift a little as the volunteers spoke with those who wanted to talk, read Bible stories to those who seemed able to comprehend, or simply knelt beside the beds of others and soothingly caressed the foreheads of men who seemed incapable of responding, or were too despondent to move. The young people moved among the men with indescribable love and joy. The atmosphere of the dreary ward was transformed and became almost family-like. In fact the young people were the only 'family' that most of these discarded men knew. They clung to the attention and love. Never have I seen such grace in action. It was infectious.

By the time the Communion table had been prepared, chairs and stools arranged, and the motley group assembled, the atmosphere was charged with a palpable sense of Christ's presence. Eyes that had been distant and vacant now seemed to sparkle with anticipation. The service commenced. What followed was, for me, one of the most memorable and moving experiences of God's love being poured out in the ruins of human existence. There was no doubt that, among all of the other men in that prison, Jesus Christ was present for the most ruined of them all.

The following day, the chaplain, several of the young people ,and I met with the local archbishop who is considered one of the great scholars of the church. He received us warmly and we had a delightful discussion concerning our visit to the prison the previous day.

'I have spent my whole life in the church,' observed the archbishop quietly. 'I know the church inside out. I have studied the doctrines of the church, and I have studied the structures and the history of the church through the ages. But it was when I visited that prison that I encountered the living church. I saw the church alive in the love of the volunteers caring for those sick prisoners in the name of Christ.'

As the archbishop reflected on the experience of his own visit to the prison and of seeing the living church, I realized how wrong my initial feelings of disappointment had been in response to that 'useless' group of inmates. I 'knew,' as we entered the medical ward, that we could surely do better by getting involved with the inmate leaders. Why on earth spend valuable time with men in the ruins of their existence? How much more strategic would it be to affect the prison by focusing our attention on more 'normal' criminals?

I was totally off base, for God's love is often expressed most powerfully amid the ruins of human existence. The strength of His love brings life amid decay, and vitality amid weakness. The living church is always a church that embraces the weakest, the feeblest, and the most incompetent. The Easter truth is the resurrection of a dead man, Jesus. This reality is reiterated wherever and whenever His love and life is poured out through His people, as they for others, in the decaying, forgotten ruins of humanity. This is the church, the community of the resurrection, people loving as God loves amidst the ruins of the world.

God's love doesn't simply follow me where I desire to go, but sometimes leads me into smelly, rotten, dismal, ruined places I'd just as soon avoid.

The Spirit of the Lord is on me,
    because he has anointed me
    to preach good news to the poor.
He has sent me to proclaim freedom for the prisoners
    and recovery of sight for the blind,
to release the oppressed,
    to proclaim the year of the Lord's favor (Luke 4:18-19).

13

BAREFOOT WALKS COMPASSION

Eight women were making their way painstakingly up a stony, dusty, rutted road toward the old prison at the top of the hill. I watched them, somewhat disinterestedly, from the comfort of an air-conditioned van. Their trek was obviously arduous, the effort compounded by the loads they were carrying on top of their heads and the stifling heat of the midday African sun. I was consciously grateful for the cool air blowing on my face. I couldn't imagine why anyone would choose to be outside under the blazing sun at this time of day. As the women reached the top of the hill, I suddenly noticed that they weren't wearing any shoes. They were completely barefoot, and their feet were scarred.

The cry of 'It's them,' interrupted my thoughts as someone jumped from the van and ran down the road to greet them. 'They're the prison visitors,' someone at the back of the van said. 'They're coming to feed the prisoners.'

We all got out of the van and stood together at the prison entrance waiting for an officer to come and unlock the huge steel gates. 'There is much suffering in here,' one of the barefoot women told me as I asked about her visit. 'We come here almost every day to make food for those who are starving.' As I chatted with the women my curiosity gave way to sheer amazement. Seldom have I been so humbled by the compassion of people who serve the poorest of the poor. To describe them as 'self-sacrificing' in their care for the prisoners scarcely begins to tell the story, for the women were themselves very poor and faced some difficulty in providing for their own families. But when they heard about prisoners dying of hunger, abandoned by their own families and relatives, they felt that they could not stand by and do nothing. They felt outraged that men should be forced to suffer such inhumanity, even if they were offenders.

The old prison was indeed in terrible condition. It was old, dingy, dilapidated, and overcrowded. Ragged prisoners milled about in stifling, dirty courtyards. Here and there, small groups of prisoners tended to small, smoky fires over which they were cooking whatever scraps of food they had. Others languished in the hot shade, too tired and weak to move. Most of them would go hungry except for the single meal a day prepared for them by the visitors. Hundreds of inmates had already died from malnutrition and disease, and the women were trying as best they could to feed those in greatest danger.

The living conditions in the prison were as bad as I had ever seen. The unpainted wooden structures used for housing the inmates were seriously dilapidated. Several years ago a tropical cyclone severely damaged the roofs of the buildings and since then, when it rained, there was as much water inside as out. Malarial mosquitoes and swarms of other insects added to the discomfort. Tiers of rickety, wooden platforms on which the prisoners slept elbow-to-elbow and toe-to-toe left room for nothing else in the barracks. A few inmates were fortunate enough to have a piece of cardboard or an old, worn-out blanket for covering. Most had nothing. The only possession most prisoners had was whatever clothing they were wearing. Most of them wore buttonless shirts and short pants that were threadbare and tattered.

My heart went out to them, even as anger welled up against the inhumanity of a system that could place people in such disastrous conditions.

The prison infirmary was grotesque. Yet in spite of little space, almost no medical supplies, and no running water, it offered a meager respite for those who were the sickest and dying. I saw men groaning in agony, their bodies wracked by untreated disease made worse by the lack of nutrition. Some men had tuberculosis and were dying a slow death, their limbs swollen, distorted, and discolored. I also saw the embarrassment and pain in the eyes of the prison staff who wanted to help but had neither the means nor the power to do so. They, too, were prisoners of the politics and economy of the country.

By the time I left the prison's infirmary I was overwhelmed and depressed by the misery of it all. The only glimmer of hope I saw walked on bare feet – the feet of the poor women, prison visitors, stirring pots of soup in a makeshift bamboo lean-to in the prison yard. They were hard at work yet smiling and chatting with the prisoners as they cooked up the rice and vegetables they'd carried all the way from town. Clearly theirs was a labor of love: love for Christ and love for the suffering prison inmates. Not one of the women was there because they had to be, and every one of them would have been justified in staying at home to look after their own needs and those of their families. They were poor. They literally had no shoes, and if they could have afforded shoes they would have spent the money to buy rice for the prisoners instead. What, after all, is the discomfort of walking on bare feet when the men in prison are suffering without food?

The memory of those barefoot prison visitors, members of Prison Fellowship, serving rice and soup to prisoners, will remain with me forever.

Unlike the 'good' work I do, no one was paying them to care, nor did some benefactor fund their modest feeding program. They were serving prisoners out of love for God – God's love within them, giving of their own necessities and even walking barefoot so that the men could eat.

That night when I returned to my clean bed and air-conditioned hotel room I could not sleep. It wasn't the first time. The pain I felt did not resolve itself, for it is too easy to live in a world of relative comfort and plenty in the face of such excruciating needs at home and around the world. When the suffering of others is out of sight it is also often out of mind, and my own needs and wants begin to dominate. I feel convicted of my selfishness when I think of the compassion and generosity of those barefoot women.

If compassion is the ability to 'feel with' or to 'suffer with' the pain of another person, those women exuded genuine compassion. They didn't just feel sorry for the prisoners or empathize with their condition. Those bare feet said it all.

I've often heard the saying that to truly understand someone or other, it is necessary to 'walk a mile in their shoes.' While I can't begin to imagine how a loving Heavenly Father feels when He sees his children suffering and hears their groaning, I think those women do – for they, like God, walk amongst the miserable and the suffering of the world on their own bare feet.

I doubt very much that it would be helpful for me to show up in London or Washington, Baghdad or Katmandu, walking barefoot through the streets. But I have begun to realize that loving as Christ loves involves more than simply being a spare-time helper or a surplus giver.

Therefore, as God's chosen people, holy and dearly loved, clothe yourselves with compassion, kindness, humility, gentleness and patience. Bear with each other and forgive whatever grievances you may have against one another. Forgive as the Lord forgave you. And over all these virtues put on love, which binds them all together in perfect unity (Col. 3:12-14).

14

CHRISTIANITY AND RELIGION

I have been thinking about the great religions of the world – Islam, Buddhism, Hinduism, and Christianity – wondering why, in the study of religion, Christianity is treated on par with other religions. All of my life I have simply assumed Christianity as the one true religion and the others not. But lately I've been wondering, as far as religion is concerned, if Christianity is really anything more than just a different religion.

I'm trying to imagine how people from other religious traditions see Christians. If I could see Christianity through their eyes, what would I see? Would I see a religion that reflects the highest ideals of its namesake (Jesus Christ) or would I see something different? Would I see people united in and by their common faith, or would I see that Christians are often just as polarized and prejudiced by race, economics, politics, and ideology as the rest of society? And if I studied the variations of Christian theology, would I find myself confused and overwhelmed by the great lengths to which Christians go in defining and differentiating themselves from other Christians?

Without question, the political and social history of Christianity is interwoven with the tragedy of divisiveness and conflict. The way people from other religions often view Christians, they appear to be fragmented and competitive, if not combative. Even on Sunday mornings, when Christians gather to pay their respects to Jesus, they do so in 'tribal' enclaves separated by race, and style, and doctrinal creeds.

There are innumerable varieties of Christians, each claiming Jesus as Lord and that He is the God who is present among them. Of course, it would be most difficult for anyone from another religion to figure out who among Christians has the rightful claim on Jesus. If Jesus Christ was the archetypal or first Christian, one might wonder which kind of Christian He might have been. Would He have been Pentecostal, Orthodox, Roman Catholic, Methodist, Anglican, Southern Baptist, Conservative Baptist, Bible Baptist, Nazarene, Seventh Day Adventist, Church of God, Church of Christ, Church of God in Christ, Wesleyan, Congregational, Uniting, Foursquare, Full Gospel, Presbyterian, Bible Church, or, perhaps, 'mega-church-nondenominational-independent'?

It's as confusing for insiders as for folks who are outsiders to Christianity. I've had to come to a conclusion that Jesus wasn't a Christian and that He didn't actually found the Christian religion. My response to people outside the Christian faith is that the good news about Jesus had nothing to do with the formation of a new religion, but that it was about God being so in love with humankind that He came to live and walk as one of them in order to save them from sin. Jesus was not a Christian. He was the Christ – God, out of sheer love, coming into the ruins of humanity as a man, as God in human flesh to live and die as one of us. The best news of all is that the chains and finality of death could not hold Him. He broke the bondage of sin and death in order to free humanity from guilt (forgiveness) and to give them a glorious hope and a future.

The amazing story of Jesus the Christ stands over and against the story of mere religion. It is the story of God's loving, forgiving, and saving embrace of humankind. Everywhere Jesus went, people flocked to be touched by His kindness and to be healed of their diseases. Where religion imposed rigid legalism, Jesus proclaimed a new lifestyle of love. Where religion excluded those whose beliefs and practices did not conform, Jesus went out of His way to include the impure, unacceptable, and uncared for Jesus Christ was the gracious embodiment of God's unconditional love.

I think it is a tragedy that the life and teachings of Jesus Christ have been devolved into a religion, Christianity, which bears His name but obscures His fantastic reality with all of the accoutrements of religion. It was never by intent, but through the collective force of pride and politics and prejudice by which we tend to create systems, institutions, and ideologies for ourselves.

Like Jesus Himself, the first disciples and early followers of Jesus did not intend to form a new religion. They simply worshipped Jesus and tried to live as He had taught them to live. They became known for their Jesus-like lifestyle and were nicknamed Christians. It came about as growing numbers of people believed in Jesus Christ and began living their lives according to His love and teachings that persecution broke out against them for not conforming to the dominant religion and politics of the day. Under persecution these followers of Jesus remained convinced and true to their belief in Him and devoted to His teachings. Historians suggest that it was not these believers who called themselves Christians, but those nonbelievers observing their visible kinship and fidelity to Jesus, who referred to them as Christians, not because they were religious, but because they lived like 'little Christs.' Their lifestyle and love reflected Jesus Christ.

> [M]en from Cyprus and Cyrene, went to Antioch and began to speak to Greeks also, telling them the good news about the Lord Jesus. The Lord's hand was with them, and a great number of people believed and turned to the Lord. News of this reached the ears of the church at Jerusalem, and they

sent Barnabas to Antioch. When he arrived and saw the evidence of the grace of God, he was glad and encouraged them all to remain true to the Lord with all their hearts. He was a good man, full of the Holy Spirit and faith, and a great number of people were brought to the Lord. Then Barnabas went to Tarsus to look for Saul, and when he found him, he brought him to Antioch. So for a whole year Barnabas and Saul met with the church and taught great numbers of people. The disciples were called Christians first at Antioch (Acts 11:20-26).

15

JESUS FREAKS

I was studying in the university during the height of the so-called 'hippie' era (free love, anti-war protests and love-ins, the emerging drug scene, and varieties of anti-establishment countercultural movements). It was during the same time that the 'Jesus People' came on the scene – a hippie-like movement whose adherents we referred to as the 'Jesus Freaks.'

At first, the Jesus Freaks seemed to me like they were just another version of being hippie – hippies who liked Jesus. I soon discovered, however, that many of them had actually been real hippies and had opted out of the mainstream culture into drugs, free sex, and experimentation with Eastern religions. In the midst of all of their experimentation they encountered Jesus Christ – not the Jesus of 'big business' religion or the establishment church, but the humble Jesus of the Gospels who wore sandals like they did and talked of freedom, peace, love, and justice; and who Himself appeared as a countercultural and anti-establishment figure.

These hippies discovered a new 'high' in Jesus and His message. Their lives became transformed as they experienced the power of Jesus setting them free from drugs and filling their lives with a sense of love more satisfying than libertine free sex and social freedom had ever been. Their hippie-like lives reflected in a vibrancy of faith, joy, and hope during a time of growing cultural cynicism and conflict. Yet most of the Jesus Freaks did not fit in well with establishment Christianity. They wore sandals; had long hair; flashed 'one way' signs; strummed guitars; sang counter-cultural songs about peace and love; and shied away from dogma, ritual, and church formalities.

The press referred to them as the Jesus People and treated them as more of a curiosity than as people to be taken seriously. Yet the accounts of personal transformation, beach-side baptisms, and recovery from drug dependency and other addictions continued. In the ethos of the times, this was good news even though the church found it difficult to accommodate their exuberant free-form worship, rock music, long hair, and casual appearance. The Jesus Freaks were nonconformist; they simply didn't connect with the 'dead' forms and institutions of organized Christianity.

Recently an article in our local newspaper reminded me of the Jesus Freaks. It was an odd article accompanied by a photo of a young man referred to as having a resemblance to Jesus. He was an odd, strange-looking, long-haired, bearded, barefoot, blanket-robed young man who showed up out of 'nowhere' on the streets of a nearby town. His life was as mysterious as his appearance. Reluctant to speak about himself, reporters were unable to learn much from him except for his name and his desire to be like Jesus. The article went on to describe him as a 'Jesus-like' person who looks like Jesus and sounds like Jesus and who has a profoundly positive impact on the people he meets. People who had been ill reported that they began feeling better when they met him. Youths with behavior problems had begun to turn their lives around, and people spoke of a palpable sense of community well-being that seemed to follow his wake.

This 'Jesus' person was described as being a gentle and humble man who walked from place to place, carried no suitcase, and sought no funding. He was totally dependent on the hospitality of strangers, stayed in places where he felt welcomed, and moved on when he felt unwelcome. People in the community were captivated by him and described him as having a 'holy' presence. Wherever he went, young and old alike felt attracted to him and sought him out for advice and conversation. Interviews with local clergy seemed to confirm that his message was consistent with the teachings of Jesus.

I found myself sharing the underlying cynicism and skepticism reflected in some of the news articles. Investigative reporters discovered that his name was Carl Joseph, born and raised in the USA, and that he had a police record. It seemed to some people that he was a rather unlikely candidate for sainthood. Yet Carl Joseph, a man with a disjointed past, had an encounter with Jesus Christ that completely changed his life. He decided to leave everything in order to literally follow Jesus. In an interview a reporter suggested that his literal Jesus-like appearance simply might be a gimmick to attract attention to himself, while another suggested that he was verging on being cultish and manipulative.

Truthfully, I don't understand why Carl Joseph would want to dress and look like Jesus in the modern world. It seems so irresponsible and out of touch with reality to be walking from town to town without any means of support, and living an itinerant lifestyle similar to that of the disciples sent out by Jesus two thousand years ago. It is all quite interesting, even amusing, but weird – out of step with the times and the culture, a bit reminiscent of the Jesus Freaks. But when I listened carefully to Carl Joseph's message, I heard the words of a man who seemed to love Jesus deeply, and his message had the ring of authenticity.

Isn't it odd that a man who decides to follow Jesus so literally is having such an impact on the lives of people and the community? People are captivated by him, for in him they encounter something they are hungry for. It seems that many of them actually experience the unconditional, non-threatening, presence of Jesus – not the domesticated Jesus of the uncomfortable pew and dogmatic denominational frameworks, but the humble Jesus who once visited towns and villages and who touched and cared for ordinary people where they lived. His message was startling in its simplicity. His love was refreshingly sincere, and the touch of His presence brought peace and life. Carl Joseph's life seems to reflect this love and peace of Jesus Christ. He is what I'd still call a Jesus Freak! Carl Joseph is countercultural but his life exudes the humility, compassion, and love of Jesus.

So I've been wondering what our towns, villages, and cities would be like if all of us Christians were to quit sitting around in our churches and walk into the shopping areas, parks, and neighborhoods acting just a little bit more like Jesus Freaks. What if, every day, we were to make a point of thinking a little more like Jesus thought, speaking a little more like Jesus spoke, and acting just a little more like Jesus did?

> If you have any encouragement from being united with Christ, if any comfort from his love, if any fellowship with the Spirit, if any tenderness and compassion, then make my joy complete by being like-minded, having the same love, being one in spirit and purpose. Do nothing out of selfish ambition or vain conceit, but in humility consider others better than yourselves. Each of you should not look only to your own interests, but also to the interests of others. Your attitude should be the same as that of Christ Jesus... (Phil. 2:1-5).

16

MIND THE GAP

Immanuel Kant, philosopher of the eighteenth century, wrote, 'Out of timber as crooked as that which man is made of, nothing perfectly straight can be carved.' Having spent most of my life working among criminal offenders and prisoners, I am all too familiar with the crooked timber of humanity. While some of that timber is visibly distorted and grotesque, I am not unaware of the subtle warp and woof in the timber of my own being.

Charles Darwin shocked the world with his radical notion of the evolution of the species – that human beings are the logical offspring of apes. 'If that is the case,' a person reportedly asked him on one occasion, 'is there anything at all unique about being human?' Darwin simply replied, 'Man is the only animal that blushes.' Unlike any other animal species, we *Homo sapiens* (human beings) are endowed with the ability to recognize the gap between what we do or are, and what we are expected to do or to be.[1] We have the capacity to blush, to be embarrassed by the gap between our actual behavior and what our behavior

---

[1] Harold S. Kushner, *How Good do we Have to be?* (New York: Little Brown & Co., 1996), p. 35.

should have been. Human beings feel guilt not just for failing to live up to the expectations of others, but especially in failing to measure up to the level of moral and spiritual perfection that we think God expects of us. We live as creatures that are aware and mindful of the gap.

My involvement with criminal offenders is all about this gap. I work with people who try to close the gap between what they do and what they know they should do, and I work with those who have chosen to ignore the gap. One of the most crucial questions human beings contend with is how to handle the gap. In situations of moral failings, misdeeds, failings, and sin, people try to cover up the gap, deny it, explain and rationalize it, struggle to overcome it, or eventually look for help to resolve it.

My own tendency has been to try lifting myself up by my moral bootstraps again and again. But my life sometimes seems to seesaw back and forth between doing what I know I ought not to do, and not doing what I resolve to do and know that I ought to do.

In the fourth century, Prudentius proposed a list of 'Seven Contrary Virtues' as an antidote to protect oneself against the 'Seven Deadly Sins.' He prescribed the following contrary virtues:

- Humility to defend yourself against pride.
- Kindness to protect yourself from envy.
- Abstinence to prevent yourself from gluttony.
- Chastity to guard yourself against lust.
- Patience to prevent yourself from anger.
- Generosity to protect yourself from covetousness.
- Diligence to keep yourself from sloth.

Pre-Christian classical Greek philosophers likewise focused on defining cardinal virtues (from the Greek *cardo*, meaning 'hinge') as the basis for social civility and upright character. According to them, the four cardinal virtues necessary for virtuous living were prudence, temperance, courage, and justice. These were later modified by the Christian church as being justice, mercy, fortitude, and prudence, which were undergirded by the addition of three theological virtues – love, hope, and faith.

Yet as much as we humans have been able to define what is virtuous, we seem unable to make ourselves consistently virtuous. We are unable to close the gap and we live with a nagging realization that no matter how diligently we try, we cannot become consistently good, at least not good enough for God. The ultimate results of this sense of futility are evident in the prisons of the world. I see this so clearly among offenders who have resigned themselves to living with the gap (it's just the way they are); those who have given up trying to cross the gap (I can't help myself); those who have tried to blind themselves to the existence of the gap through uninhibited self-indulgence and escapism (I can't deal with this); and those who defy the reality of the gap (I don't care!).

But the question still remains: can any of us cross the gap? How good do we have to be? I've come to realize that these are the wrong questions. Mind the gap – yes – but the gap we cannot close has been closed by the Heavenly Father who forgives us when we fail, and who helps us when we cannot help ourselves. None of us has to go it alone, and the gap is not too wide for any of us to receive the Father's help.

> I know that nothing good lives in me, that is, in my sinful nature. For I have the desire to do what is good, but I cannot carry it out. For what I do is not the good I want to do; no, the evil I do not want to do – this I keep on doing. Now if I do what I do not want to do, it is no longer I who do it, but it is sin living in me that does it. So I find this law at work: When I want to do good, evil is right there with me. For in my inner being I delight in God's law; but I see another law at work in the members of my body, waging war against the law of my mind and making me a prisoner of the law of sin at work within my members. What a wretched man I am!

Who will rescue me from this body of death? Thanks be to God – through Jesus Christ our Lord! So then, I myself in my mind am a slave to God's law, but in the sinful nature a slave to the law of sin. Therefore, there is now no condemnation for those who are in Christ Jesus, because through Christ Jesus the law of the Spirit of life set me free from the law of sin and death (Rom. 7:18–8:2).

17

IF LOOKS COULD KILL...

Everything about the man was irritating. The way he walked displayed an attitude of superiority that totally grated on my nerves. As the usher escorted us to the pew where he was sitting, I indicated my preference for another seat just a little further down the aisle. It is not that I had even so much as spoken to the man; I just knew I didn't want to sit anywhere near him. His mannerisms annoyed me so greatly that it was difficult to concentrate on the service.

Several weeks ago I happened to be sitting right behind him during the service and my irritation grew increasingly intense with each hymn, Scripture reading, prayer, and even during the sermon. By the time of the benediction I had written the man off as despicable even though I hadn't exchanged so much as a word with him.

So when I saw him seated in church the following Sunday I made certain to sit in a place where he would be out of my direct view. Even so, I felt annoyed. The man's shifty mannerisms irritated me to no end. It was obvious to me that he was an arrogant and obnoxious individual. Settling into the pew, I was relieved that I would be able to pray and worship without having him anywhere near me. Then during the prayers I heard someone, I'm sure the voice was his, repeating the prayer about two very irritating syllables ahead of the rest of the congregation. His pace was even worse as we recited the Creed. By now the fangs of my anger were completely exposed. I flashed an angry look over my shoulder and sure enough it was him! 'If he can't participate properly, he ought to get out,' I muttered angrily to myself, and then sheepishly hoped that the folks in the pew ahead of me hadn't heard.

During Communion I made my way to the altar to partake of the bread and wine – the Body and Blood of Christ. As the bread and wine were distributed to each in turn I was struck by the idea that there is only one Body and one Blood, and that each of us who comes to the altar partake of that Body and Blood – and that we are members of that same Body!

Time seemed frozen as I realized that I was kneeling among sinners at the altar sharing the 'holy meal' with the likes of them. I had no idea who most of them were but in all likelihood there were probably a few liars, an adulterer or two, a couple of alcoholics, a homosexual, and certainly a few gossips and a variety of other sinners. I was kneeling with some heavy-duty sinners to share the Body and Blood of Christ. I was appalled by the thought as I looked around and noticed the fellow who irritated me so much.

The chalice was raised to my lips. 'Drink this in remembrance that Christ's blood was shed for you, and be thankful,', the minister intoned. I hesitated as the realization dawned on me – along with all of the other sinners at the altar was one whose heart and mind were poisoned against a man he'd never met. As I drank from the cup I realized that, if looks could kill, I'd just killed another man.

Kneeling together in recognition of our common humanity and need, we confessed our weakness and dependence on the One whose body was broken and whose blood was spilled for guilty sinners. I had come feeling superior to the others and better by far than the man who irritated me so much. But in that moment I realized that I was no better in my guilt than any of my brothers and sisters. Together, in our thirst, we drank deeply from the fount of grace.

'God deliver me from my pride,', I prayed. 'Help me to see myself for who I am and to live in harmony and love with all the other sinners for whom you died, those with whom I share your life.'

Is not the cup of thanksgiving for which we give thanks a participation in the blood of Christ? And is not the bread that we break a participation in the body of Christ? Because there is one loaf, we, who are many, are one body, for we all partake of the one loaf (1 Cor. 10:16-17).

18

I'm Okay – I Really Am

When I compare myself to certain other people I can actually feel quite good about myself. That sounds rather crass, doesn't it? Yet it's true. Haven't you noticed how the world seems to have more than its share of people who tend to be incompetent, lazy, and insensible. I have only to compare myself to individuals who manifest those traits in order to feel rather pleased with my own condition and progress in life. I feel good about being competent, taking initiative, and using my God-given common sense.

I realize, of course, that the world is full of inequality and that not everyone has an equal opportunity. I am also painfully aware of the fact that there are moral differences between people. Some people seem naturally to be more self-indulgent and insensitive, or morally indecent, or hostile and hateful. When I think about myself in relation to drug peddlers and addicts, wife beaters and child molesters, tax cheats and business frauds, or to the purveyors of sexual promiscuity and perversion, I almost feel pure. My petty little vices fade into the background by comparison to the gross moral decadence around me.

When I compare myself to other people it is not too difficult to begin feeling satisfied with my condition. I suppose I am 'blessed' because in many ways God has both gifted me for good and protected me from evil. Gratitude fills my heart when I look around and recognize that, unlike many people, I know where my goodness comes from. I don't take pride in this, for it is indeed by the grace of God that I am neither slothful nor perverted. My heart surges with thanksgiving when I compare myself to the messy lives of even some of my close friends. I wonder however, in giving thanks, if I am not also prone to congratulating myself for being me.

But this 'thanksgiving' is somewhat suspect because I know it isn't pure. While I am certainly thanking God for the blessings I've received, I also know that some of the satisfaction I feel arises out of a downward comparison of myself to other people. The source of feeling good about myself often comes from looking down on other people instead of humbly looking up toward Christ. In looking down on other people I am elevating myself, but when I look up at Jesus Christ I realize that I am really not so good at all.

In looking up to Jesus I become aware of the wolves of selfishness and pride howling in the outback of my soul. I become aware of my reluctant faltering steps in doing the things I know I should do and in refraining from doing the things I know I shouldn't do, or think, or say. In truth, the people I compare myself to are probably more honest than I am; for what you see in their lives is what you get, while I have pride fully cloaked with decency and spirituality.

So am I really as okay as I'd like to think I am? Of course I am, but it is not relative to my goodness compared to others; it is only a consequence of God's love and grace. Why should I be so greatly blessed to grow up in a wonderful family, in a peaceful country, and a prosperous community? Why should I be so greatly blessed to have access to a good education, good friends, and great opportunities? Why should I be blessed with robust health and a good life? I can only thank God for all of these benefits, and in doing so I know it has nothing to do with being better than other people – it is about being undeservedly blessed. I am amazed that God has blessed me. The only okay thing I can do is humbly to thank Him, and to love Him in return by loving my fellow man.

To some who were confident of their own righteousness and looked down on everybody else, Jesus told this parable: 'Two men went up to the temple to pray, one a Pharisee and the other a tax collector. The Pharisee stood up and prayed about himself: 'God, I thank you that I am not like other men – robbers, evildoers, adulterers – or even like this tax collector...' But the tax collector stood at a distance. He would not even look up to heaven, but beat his breast and said 'God have mercy on me, a sinner.' I tell you that this man, rather than the other, went home justified before God' (Luke 18:9-11, 13-14).

19

WHO'S THE FAIREST OF THEM ALL?

I wonder if any of us are really as good as we sometimes think we are? Don't get me wrong, I know that most of us have struggled with issues of inadequacy even as we've grown older. We've felt the heavy weight of our failures and shortcomings, and have tried hard to improve or at least to minimize the appearance of our failures. Recently, however, I've been plagued by an uncomfortable and contrary thought. Perhaps it is something that emerged as a by-product of my preoccupation with helping people who have failed miserably and in most cases visibly – or maybe it is just a dark premonition that lurks just beneath our consciousness.

What I've begun to realize is that I've become self-satisfied with the goodness of my own life and work in comparison to the bums, beggars, and boneheads of the world. My work is an extension of myself – I take great satisfaction in helping people who are in trouble, people who cannot seem to help themselves. Being able to make a positive difference, a good contribution to their lives, has become a source of great satisfaction. I take pride in the fact that the organization I work for is innovative and successful. We are reaching people at the bottom of the 'social heap' in countries that are at the bottom of the 'economic heap.' We are involved in leading a unique and influential movement. We are terrific – and I am part of that. Wow!

Yet my mind drifts back into the hidden shadow of my own bumbling, stumbling ways. I don't get stuck there because it is clear to me that God's grace has kept me out of the pit of many things. But in a troubling sense I think God had pretty good raw material to work with when He chose to smile upon me. Sure, I've made more mistakes than I can remember, and there have been some big ones I'm too embarrassed even to talk about in the dark. Notwithstanding my past and occasional lapses in the present, I live on the unspoken assumption that, in the balance of things, my sinful disposition really isn't as bad as most. I certainly could be worse.

My chest swells with worth when I think about all of the good things that I've been doing – the down-and-out people I've helped, the great programs I've initiated, the positive influence I've had on my colleagues and friends. I'm rather pleased with what I've accomplished. It is a kind of self-satisfaction that is neither complacent nor lethargic. It's rooted in my need to prove my worth by helping those 'beneath' me. I am an achiever and like most achievers I am proud of my ability to make good things happen.

I've been thinking a lot about this and what's becoming clear to me is that, like the people I am helping, I have a serious problem and I cannot help myself. In reality my problem is probably baser and more pervasive than the problems of addiction, anger, avarice – it is the problem of my fatal attraction to myself. For when I feel best about myself – most competent, most gratified – a subtle shift of focus takes place and soon the center of my spiritual universe is me: it's all about my work, my ideas, my vision, my impact and all the good that I am doing.

Like an addict who can't let go, or like an angry person whose outburst brings no peace, or like a person whose greed knows no satiety, those of us who admire the fountain of our own prowess, performance, and piety worship a falling god. Of all the things that lead to sin and evil, pride is the basest temptation of them all.

> 'But my people have exchanged their Glory
>> for worthless idols.
> Be appalled at this, O heavens,
>> and shudder with great horror,'
>>> declares the LORD.
> 'My people have committed two sins:
> They have forsaken me,
>> the spring of living water,
> and have dug their own cisterns,
>> broken cisterns that cannot hold water (Jer. 2:11b-13).

20

HOUSE OF THE LIVING DEAD

Some years ago I met Alexander Ginzburg, who was a dissident Russian poet during the era of repression. For more than nine years he had been a prisoner of conscience in one of the harshest strict regime labor camps of the Soviet Union – Mordovian Camp No. 1. Ginzburg impressed me as a man of deep faith and conviction who had weathered much indignity, deprivation, and cruelty for his refusal to be silent in the face of political and social injustice. The price he paid was exacted in emotional anguish and brutalizing physical labor. Like others who have somehow managed to survive the tortuous reality of such imprisonment, words are not adequate to describe the miseries he endured – but hope saw him through.

During the nineteenth century one of the greatest Russian authors, Fyodor Dostoevsky, was imprisoned as a 'traitor' during the tsarist regime. He referred to his prison experience as being confined in 'the house of the living dead.' Writing about his imprisonment in a brutal labor camp, Dostoevsky graphically depicts the bleak, painful, soul-wrenching existence of people held captive without dignity, worth, and purpose – where prisoners are reduced to aching empty shells of humanity entombed in conditions that extinguish life and hope.

Most prisons, to a greater or lesser degree, reek of despair and death. There is little hope in these pits of hell, particularly among inmates who have no meaningful thread of family or faith to hang on to. A 'Good Friday' pall of depressive hopelessness slowly suffocates them – there is no way out. Yet it is precisely in such pits, at the bitter end of human possibility, that the good news of the resurrection is most dramatic. When people suffer in a hopeless oppressive void, in a place of living death, only the miracle of resurrection can transform their dread.

Yet for many people in prison, as for many people out of prison, the hope of Christ's resurrection, the Easter drama, seems too other-worldly to be real. In our sophisticated techno-world, belief in an 'Easter' hope and victory – a cosmic resurrection from decay and death – is often relegated to the dustbins of fantasy and the unenlightened past. In some parts of the world, belief in the reality of the God of Easter is regarded as undermining the supremacy of the state and the powers that be. That certainly was the situation Ginzburg and his colleagues experienced under the domination of the Soviet state.

I was acutely aware of the notoriety of Soviet prisons as I stepped anxiously through the steel gates of a large prison outside of Moscow during the final years of the Soviet empire. Knowing how so many people of faith had been tortured and killed at the hands of the Soviets, I was more than a little apprehensive about visiting prison in the company of a few courageous Christians. Our visit began not unlike prison visits I've made in more than 100 other countries. We met with the officers in charge of the prison, drank tea with them, and then toured the facilities. It happened to be a bright spring day that contrasted with the foreboding grey walls and drab appearance of the inmates. Very few of them looked me in the eye and when they did they averted my smile with a downward glance and stooped shoulders. I could feel their gloom and pain. Yet every once in a while a prisoner would return my smile and would stop to speak with us. They were different, rising above the dreariness, and I felt a buoyancy of joy and love.

Our visit ended in a big hall where prisoners were frequently assembled for political retraining and rehabilitation lectures. Recently, due to the emerging liberalization of Soviet policy, the hall had also been used for an unprecedented religious gathering. For a special occasion a church group had been allowed to present a musical concert and program for the inmates. As I spoke with a few of the prisoners they told me about Easter Sunday and how the hall had been packed out to celebrate the Resurrection of Jesus – it had been a first for them – and it had brought 'good news'!

As I listened to the prisoners it seemed to me that they had become infected with the hope of resurrection, infected with joy and with hope – hope within the 'house of the living dead.' No wonder some of the prisoners were smiling when there was literally nothing to smile about, no wonder I could see the love of Christ in their eyes in spite of prison desolation. Resurrection was breaking through the gloom of their Good Friday existence. Jesus Christ, risen from the dead, had become their fellow prisoner, with them in their suffering and lifting their eyes beyond the guard towers and the pain.

Surely if the Resurrection means anything for any of us it means hope amid the suffocating realities of imprisonment – whether that imprisonment is defined by four stone walls and iron bars, or by personal rejection, embarrassing failure, or helpless disability. Resurrection is nothing less than hope for all of us who are, in one way or another, suffering in the 'house of the living dead.'

Praise be to the God and Father of our Lord Jesus Christ! In his great mercy he has given us new birth into a living hope through the resurrection of Jesus Christ from the dead, and into an inheritance that can never perish, spoil or fade... In this you greatly rejoice, though now for a little while you may have had to suffer grief in all kinds of trials (1 Pet. 1:3-4, 6).

21

One Bright Week

As spring arrives in the northern hemisphere the air is charged with the vitality of new life, the scent of budding trees, colorful blossoms dancing in the light, and sounds of renewed life emerging in the marshes and woodlands. Frogs, birds, and tiny insects begin singing together in an exuberant celebration of life.

The transfiguration of winter into spring is a joyous rebirth of life, as nature emerges from the cold, austere darkness of winter into the warming light of liveliness. For me, as a northerner, Easter is the crowning jewel of springtime, not just because of the seasonal triumph of light and life over darkness and decay, but because Easter itself heralds the most vibrant and spectacular triumph of life over death. Nature cycles through seasons in which spring is the wondrous start of nature's annual renewal. But Easter represents a far more vibrant and enduring springtime of life for all mankind – the ultimate triumph of life and hope over the grip of decay and death. Resurrection!

It was during the Easter season that I spent one of the most memorable weeks of my life in Russia. My visit coincided with what Russian believers call 'Bright Week'. It is the week beginning with Easter Sunday, during which joyful celebration of Christ's resurrection transcends the simple human joy associated with the emergence of spring.

Holy Week has always been a spiritual high point for me. The contemplation of Jesus's passion and suffering – the pain and humiliation He experienced on the way to Golgotha, the mockery and agony He endured on the cross – causes me to tremble. But when He died, was pierced with a spear, bound up in grave clothes, and sealed securely in a tomb – when death was the final word of evil and the works of darkness – Jesus breaks its hold in a blaze of light and life. Resurrection from death – He is risen! All of the sorrow and suffering of Holy Week culminates in death, and then God proves that He has power over death. What a celebration!

Easter Monday comes all too quickly and we go back to the routines of daily life. Our Western celebration of Easter celebration comes to climax and then it's over. Easter happened 'yesterday' and today the holy day of celebration is over. After weeks of Lenten preparation followed by the anticipation of Holy Week, the joyful noise of Resurrection Sunday gives way to another week of work.

'Bright Week' in Russia showed me that it doesn't have to be like this. After all, the Resurrection wasn't just an event that climaxed and was gone. The Resurrection dramatically and definitively signaled a new day – a whole new era. My time with Russian believers during 'Bright Week' was a continuing, joyful crescendo of Christ's resurrection that reverberated in festive liturgies and in joyful greeting. Throughout that week the first words exchanged between people in church and on the street were an exultant, 'Christ is risen!' followed by an equally exultant rejoinder, 'Christ is risen indeed!' I was amazed how the celebration of Jesus's resurrection radiated into the streets and daily life.

I was profoundly touched by this experience and came away with an overwhelming realization that the entirety of post-

Easter life is 'Bright Week.' Easter Sunday is not just the divine denouement to the story of our suffering Savior; rather it is the beginning of a celebration marking the total transformation of our human seasons – from the dark season of sin and evil into the glorious new springtime of light and life.

Much more than being an annual celebration in the cycle in the church calendar, Easter is the continuing springtime of our lives. We are living in the perpetual 'Bright Week' of resurrection life as we celebrate and live in the glory and the power of Jesus's triumph over evil and death. Jesus's resurrection didn't end with Him rising from the dead. It is the continuing drama of His victory being realized in the lives of people victimized by evil, ensnared by sin, and captive to decay and death. Yet because He overcame evil and death, we can live in the power of His resurrection, that new season of hope and joy, light and life – salvation for all humanity.

Christ is Risen!
The Lord is Risen Indeed!
Alleluia! Alleluia!

22

Jesus Christ Is Lord!

We were flying high above the earth at 10,500 meters and I felt released from the crushing helplessness I had experienced during the past few days. The stifling poverty of people living from hand to mouth, the corruption and perversity of political and government officials, and the filth of the prison receded in the horizon as we flew into the night. Heaving a huge sigh of relief, as if to exhale the accumulated tension in mind and body, I leaned comfortably back in my seat.

I closed my eyes, intending to get some rest but my heart was not at peace. I ached with the thought of so easily leaving people captive in their suffering while I was on my way back to the 'good life' of peace and plenty. How quickly I was becoming detached from the pain and suffering that they could not escape. I wondered how simplistic and shallow my expressions of concern and reassurance must have seemed to them. Confronted with the injustice of horrible prison conditions and the misery of families and young children, all I had been able to offer was compassion in the name of Jesus Christ and an affirmation of God's ultimate justice. Now, I was leaving while they remained where they were

– trapped in economic, social, and political circumstances with no human way of escape in sight.

I wondered what, if any, real difference it makes to affirm Jesus Christ as Lord in the face of such intractable injustice and inhumanity. I know that the Lordship of Jesus Christ is the core declaration of our faith. Yet high above the gritty stench of reality on the ground, it seemed almost trite for me to affirm this because I was able to leave that stench behind and would not have to live with the incongruity between the proclamation and the pain.

I have continued to ponder that incongruity. How easily the ancient and familiar proclamation, 'Jesus Christ is Lord,' rolls off my tongue. Yet how inappropriate and escapist it seems when uttered in response to people who are in anguish, drowning in a sea of helplessness and hopelessness. Where no human solution is evident, all I have been able to do is affirm that nothing anyone experiences is beyond the notice and the power of Jesus Christ. I must admit that even to me, this sometimes feels like an escape from reality or a trivialization of human suffering, and I struggle with that.

It is very difficult to understand the practical implications of proclaiming Jesus Christ as Lord in the face of trouble, turmoil, and tragedy. There is no simple answer to the seeming discontinuity between day-to-day reality and the declaration of Christ's victory over evil. I cling to hope, however, in something that transcends the finality of human degradation, disease, and even death. The proclamation that Jesus Christ is Lord is not escape from reality. It is the very heart of Christian witness in the depths of human helplessness, confronting every injustice, inhumanity, corruption, and exploitation with the declaration that it will not last and that justice and peace will ultimately triumph.

Jesus Christ is Lord! This is the proclamation of the good news of the Kingdom. It is the proclamation of hope and expectation that beyond the finite fiefdoms and powers of man is a kingdom that cannot be shaken – the Kingdom of our Lord. This proclamation revives the strength, courage, and joy of people beyond the anguish and futility of the circumstances within which they are trapped. No experience, circumstance, or station in life is the end of any person's story.

To announce that Jesus Christ is Lord among prisoners and among people in great need is to announce the good news of God's Kingdom breaking into the confines of human failure and futility. There is a future and a hope for all people.

To declare that Jesus Christ is Lord puts corrupted powers, systems, and institutions on notice that they cannot and will not last. They are temporary, for there is a higher authority and a higher power by which every nation and power will be judged. To utter the prophetic word that Jesus Christ is Lord is to confront the arrogance and evil that inhabits human systems and institutions with their own finitude.

To affirm Jesus Christ as Lord is a comforting hope in the Lord of the universe who knows sorrow, pain, and injustice. He is with those who suffer and are in need, for He is the One who knows suffering and grief; He is not a Lord who knows no pain. To proclaim Jesus Christ as Lord is also to proclaim in word and deed His presence and compassion in the anguish and ruins of human experience. To proclaim Jesus Christ as Lord is to proclaim the presence of the Savior.

Far from being an escape from reality or a trivialization of human futility and suffering, the proclamation of Jesus Christ as Lord is the proclamation of the Kingdom of God among the poor. It is the confrontation of the powers of injustice and evil. And it is bearing witness to the presence and compassion of Jesus Christ, Lord and Savior.

Jesus Christ is Lord: the One who suffered, who died, and who rose from the grave; the One who is coming again and whose Kingdom will have no end!

> [H]e will bring justice to the nations.
> He will not shout or cry out,
> > or raise his voice in the streets.

A bruised reed he will not break,
    and a smoldering wick he will not snuff out.
In faithfulness he will bring forth justice;
    he will not falter or be discouraged
till he establishes justice on earth.
    In his law the islands will put their hope.'
This is what God the LORD says –
he who created the heavens and stretched them out,
    who spread out the earth and all that comes out of it,
who gives breath to its people,
    and life to those who walk on it:
'I, the LORD, have called you in righteousness;
    I will take hold of your hand.
I will keep you and will make you
    to be a covenant for the people
    and a light for the Gentiles,
to open eyes that are blind,
    to free captives from prison
    and to release from the dungeon
        those who sit in darkness' (Isa. 42:1-7).

23

EXPERIENCING JESUS CHRIST

I have met many men and women who have come to faith in Jesus Christ while they have been serving time in prison. For some of them it was the prodigal experience of returning to the faith of their childhood and for others it was a profoundly eye-opening encounter with the reality of God's grace for the very first time. Whether their personal story is that of an errant son returning to the embrace of the Father or that of a wandering daughter, blind since birth, miraculously able to see for the first time, their stories are an inspiring and visible witness to the transforming grace of Jesus Christ.

Serge is one of those, a man who was imprisoned for more than twenty years and his story is a truly marvelous story of transformation. What struck me the very first time I met him was his spiritual vitality, the evidence of spiritual growth that continues to shine through his life and work. His life is a continuing story of transformation through Jesus Christ. As Serge and I conversed I came to realize again that the ongoing formation of a Christ-like character and lifestyle is every bit as miraculous as that profound moment when the inclination of a person's heart turns from unbelief to faith in Christ, from unrepentance to repentance, from being stultified by guilt to the exuberant release of freedom.

The life of faith is a walk, not just an experience or a belief system. The faith of Noah, Abraham, Joseph, Moses, Gideon, Elijah, St Paul, St Francis, St Patrick, William Wilberforce, William Carey, Mother Teresa, and other heroes of the faith was no mere inclination of the mind or heart. These remarkable followers of Jesus lived their faith outrageously and courageously in the face of human scandal, suffering, and sorrow.

Spiritual transformation is not simply a matter of a person changing his or her mind from unbelief to belief. While it may begin there, it is the continuing formation of values, attitudes, and lifestyle by which persons who have come to believe in Jesus learn and dare to live lives that give radical expression to their faith – often penetrating the contrary, broken, and painful world of human endeavor with the living presence of Jesus Christ.

Serge's story, like so many others, is a tremendous inspiration to me. Among the spiritually transformed prisoners and former prisoners I've met are many whose story never seems to move beyond an initial mind-changing encounter with Christ. They, like so many of us 'cradle' Christians or lifelong believers, cherish the heritage of faith and experience of Jesus Christ simply as a memory to be celebrated and remembered. For many of us, our story is like a spiritual autobiography of children who have stopped growing, moored to comfortable traditions and past experiences, going nowhere.

The ultimate miracle of experiencing Jesus Christ is the ongoing spiritual formation of a person growing in intimate relationship with Him, becoming more Christlike in the rough and tumble of everyday life. I find that this is difficult, for I too am inclined to cherish what Jesus Christ has done for me, but not always eager to experience Jesus Christ living in me. I'm naturally inclined to do my own thing. But I know that to experience the transforming reality of Jesus Christ is to enter into His life, and to be so shaped by his life, so that it is no longer I 'but Christ [who] lives in me' (Gal. 2:20).

> We are, to be sure, reconciled to God by Jesus' death, but even more. We are 'saved' by his life (Rom. 5:10) – saved in the sense of entering into his eternal kind of life, not just in some distant heaven, but right now in the midst of our broken and sorrowful world. When we carefully consider how Jesus lived while among us in the flesh, we learn how we are to live – truly live – empowered by him who is with us always even to the end of the age. We then begin an intentional 'imitatio Christi,' imitation of Christ, not in some slavish or literal fashion but by catching the spirit and power in which he lived and by learning to walk 'in his steps' (1 Pet. 2:21) (Richard Foster, *Streams of Living Water*, London: HarperCollins, 1998).

24

HOLY IN THE ORDINARY

Sometimes life feels almost like it's a tune being played on the overstretched strings of an out-of-tune violin – far too much to do with too little time – responsibilities at home competing and conflicting with responsibilities at work – a hunger for solitude at untimely odds with social obligations – joy when day breaks quickly clouded by wearying routines and pressures – personal peace with God bombarded by incessantly bad news in politics, the economy, and the environment. I'm sitting in a traffic jam at the end of another day with rush-hour traffic giving way to raucous idiotic gridlock.

'How was your day?' asks my wife as I finally extricate myself from my steamy, overheated car, disgusted with myself for not having found time to get the air-conditioning repaired. 'Oh, just fine,' I reply, knowing even as I speak that the discord between my words and mood is obvious. It's been another one of those days where the ordinary pressures of life have overtaken my consciousness of God and my sense of living in His presence.

Recently I reread a classic little book called *The Practice of the Presence of God*, based on the life of Brother Lawrence. Born Nicholas Herman in seventeenth-century France, he served as a footman and a soldier before becoming a lay brother in the order known as the 'barefoot' Carmelites. Brother Lawrence soon became acknowledged as a man who walked in the presence of God all day long. His total desire was for communion with God in all aspects, experiences, and seasons of life. For him, there was no difference between time for business and time for worship, no difference between ordinary time and holy time. In every activity of his life, even the most mundane, he cultivated a sense of God's presence.

Brother Lawrence lived his life consciously celebrating God's presence whether he was praying in the chapel or working in the monastery kitchen. 'The time of business,' he said, 'does not with me differ from the time of prayer; and in the noise and clatter of my kitchen, while several persons are at the same time calling for different things, I possess God in as great tranquility as if I were upon my knees at the blessed sacrament.' Amid all of the intrusions, interruptions, and irritations that he encountered during the day Brother Lawrence was able to keep himself always in prayer before the Lord in such a way that the clamors of life ceased being distractions from God's presence. Instead the interruptions and problems became joyful holy places where he experienced the presence of God.

Brother Lawrence's life is an illustration of what St. Paul had in mind in writing his letter to the Thessalonians, 'Be joyful always; pray continually; give thanks in all circumstances, for this is God's will for you in Christ Jesus' (1 Thess. 5:16-17). I find it awfully difficult to maintain a conscious awareness of the presence of Christ. Often the smallest intrusion, irritation, or interruption is enough to rob me of any sense of being in the presence of the Lord. Unlike Brother Lawrence, I have not been able to make a habit of praying in the face of such ordinary irritations, intrusions, and interruptions in my daily life; much less have I ever thought of giving thanks for such things.

I was pondering this recently when a colleague and I were at lunch with two men. The man I was seated next to was a long-time friend whom I had not seen for several years. As we waited to be served I found myself becoming repulsed and irritated by his bad breath, his hand constantly reaching out to touch my arm, and his invasively close sense of personal space. I kept trying to expand the distance between us but each time that I moved away from him he moved closer. I couldn't get away from him and I was on the verge of expressing my frustration at his total insensitivity and disregard for my comfort.

Finally it occurred to me that I should pray and so I offered my irritation up to the Lord, thanking Him for my friend, and thanking Him for the gift of being together – so close after so many years. During that short mental prayer I suddenly realized that I am a person who likes to keep my distance, and that what Jesus wants of me is not just to be nearby but to be closer than a brother. Jesus wants to come into my personal space – to completely invade my privacy, my comfort zone. As I was edging away from my friend, it was as if the Lord was showing me that there are times when I am also prone to edge away from Jesus, yet He keeps moving closer because He loves me and finds joy in our being together.

I was amazed how prayer, during that moment of irritation and discomfort, awakened me to a joy-filled holy experience of God's presence. It's in everyday little experiences like this – frustrating relationships, political conflict, snarled traffic, stressful work situations, family misunderstandings, and even broken airconditioners – that prayer becomes a pathway into the joy of God's presence: praying in all circumstances, thanking the Lord in all things, and listening for His voice – practicing the presence of God.

> Rejoice in the Lord always. I will say it again: Rejoice! Let your gentleness be evident to all. The Lord is near. Do not be anxious about anything, but in everything, by prayer and petition, with thanksgiving, present your requests to God. And the peace of God, which transcends all understanding, will guard your hearts and minds in Christ Jesus (Phil. 4:4-7).

25

LORD OF THE DETAILS

I woke up one morning and tried to pray; it was like swimming against the current of a madly rushing river. My mind was propelled in uncountable directions by thoughts refusing to be harnessed. Sometimes prayer is not what I want it to be: this morning was one of those times. It seemed that the connection wasn't working, and no amount of discipline seemed sufficient to keep my mind from wandering. As my thoughts raced from concern to concern I desperately tried to maintain control by forcing myself to focus on spiritual concerns. This worked for about thirty seconds and then I again found myself brooding over a work assignment, plans and preparations for an upcoming trip, my father's illness, and a host of other everyday matters.

I desired my time of prayer to be spiritually uplifting, but instead I found myself awash in a flood of mundane preoccupations. It felt as if God was a long way away, and I also found that a bit annoying. In fact it bothered me all day to the point where I became worried that there was something terribly wrong with me spiritually – something more than just being a stumbling ordinary sinner.

That evening I went home determined to sort things out, but I continued to be frustrated in my attempts to pray. In the midst of this agony it slowly began to dawn on me that perhaps I should really be praying about all the mundane details that were competing for my attention. Isn't that really what God desires – to be with me in the middle of all my petty and ordinary concerns? Being spiritual isn't just a matter of praying great prayers and thinking profound spiritual thoughts; rather it is an intimacy with God in which He shares the burden of those things that concern me and weigh me down. God is not only concerned with big issues like world peace, and justice, and the salvation of lost souls – He is concerned about me. He is the Lord of the ordinary details of life.

Mostly I am inclined to bear my lesser burdens alone. I worry about little details and brood over problems and annoyances that I have to deal with. But this is precisely where I need to let God touch my life. Perhaps the preoccupations and wandering thoughts when I try to pray are not unimportant intrusions. Maybe these are the real concerns into which I should invite God's presence and help. Real spirituality is a spirituality in which God is intimately a part of the dusty, ordinary little details of everyday life.

He is the Lord not only of the extraordinary, but of the very ordinary.

Therefore I tell you, do not worry about your life, what you will eat or drink; or about your body, what you will wear... Look at the birds of the air; they do not sow or reap or store away in barns, and yet your heavenly Father feeds them. Are you not much more valuable than they? (Matt. 6:25, 26).

26

Neighborhood Boundaries

Once upon a time we had an obnoxious, noisy neighbor who seemed to get perverse pleasure out of disturbing our peaceful, quiet weekend evenings. The man had the uncanny ability to shatter the tranquillity of our neighborhood just about when the hubbub of the day was giving way to the soft light and muted sounds of evening. Just when the rest of his neighbors were putting away their garden tools was the time he chose to begin his chores – the high-pitched whine of a leaf blower, the roar of a garden tractor, the incessant clatter of a lawn mower, the bellow of a chain saw! His untimely activities became irritatingly predictable and he personally began to grate on my nerves even though I'd only met him face to face on one occasion.

A severe snowstorm roaring out of the northeast had completely blanketed the countryside where we lived with more than a foot of snow. The roads in our neighborhood had become completely impassable. I had a flight to catch early the next morning and was desperately attempting to clear a path from our street to the main roadway, which was clear. I had begun the impossible task of shoveling my way out when the noisy

neighbor came chugging up the street with his tractor. Now there was hope! I struggled through the deep snowdrifts to the house next door where he was beginning to clear a way through the snow. I asked him if he would be able to do me a favor and clear the way to my driveway as well. Shrugging his shoulders, he looked down from his noisy perch on the tractor and curtly grunted, 'You'll have to wait; don't have time!'

Walking away in total disgust, I silently wished my neighbor all the ill luck in the world. Ironically, as I was struggling back through the snow, I heard the tractor chug and cough to a sputtering stall. Turning around I saw the tractor and driver slowly sliding off the road into the snow-covered mire of a drainage ditch. 'Couldn't have happened to a "nicer" guy,' I chuckled to myself. 'Justice is served!'

Then a sense of guilt took over, so I reluctantly picked up my shovel and retraced my steps to the now half-buried tractor to assist my struggling and unhelpful neighbor. A long while later, we managed to get the tractor out of the ditch and back onto the roadway. To my consternation he grunted 'thanks' and promptly drove the other way leaving me alone in the snow and with the way to my driveway uncleared and impassable. Admittedly, I felt an edge of anger with every recollection of this event and every time my noisy neighbor disturbed the peace of my weekend evenings. I felt like the good neighborhood we live in just didn't deserve a man like him!

Like the lawyer who wanted Jesus to define 'neighbor' for him, I also find myself struggling with the broad idea of loving my neighbor as myself. It is much more manageable and comfortable to define the boundaries of my neighborliness to encompass only the people I like and who, in turn, like me. These are natural neighborhood boundaries that may not be defined by mere geographic proximity, but by a deeper proximity that includes things such as social compatibility, emotional connectivity, shared interests, and shared beliefs. My noisy, undesirable neighbor was not included within the boundaries of that neighborhood, despite the fact that he lived nearby. In actuality, there is no real neighborliness between us except for coexistence within a geographic boundary.

When the lawyer asked Jesus, 'And who is my neighbor?' it was really not such a dumb question. It is a question that I'd like a satisfactory answer to because Jesus seems to have left the idea of loving one's neighbor wide open. What are the boundaries of my neighborhood? Who is really my neighbor? How far and under what conditions should my love and neighborliness be extended? Next door to the older divorced woman who lives alone? Across the street to the elderly retired couple? Down the street to the man who is suffering from cancer? To the end of the block to the odd, reclusive couple who keep their window shades drawn? To the foreigners several streets away whose overgrown weeds spoil the beauty of the neighborhood? To the detestable, unhelpful, noisy neighbor who refused to help me?

There is no easy answer, for I could spend my entire career befriending and caring for the people who live within the geographic boundaries of my neighborhood. But who is really my neighbor? In answer to the lawyer's question, Jesus told the story of three men who encountered a stranger in desperate need. Only one of the three men stopped to help. The other two men saw a boundary between themselves and the stranger in need, a boundary that excluded the stranger from their neighborhood and excused those two men from any obligation to help.

Which of the three men was a neighbor to the stranger in need? It is painfully obvious. It was the man whose neighborliness was not constrained by the boundaries of comfort, custom, or commonality. The real question is not, 'Who is my neighbor, or what boundaries define my neighborhood?' but rather 'Who is neighborly?'

[T]o love your neighbor as yourself is more important than all burnt offerings and sacrifices (Mark 12:33).

27

OF NAILS THAT PREACH

Almost everyone I know has an Uncle John. I did too, but my Uncle John passed away one cold January day. It was somehow fitting that he should die in the middle of a bleak Canadian winter. For an 83-year-old man to have died in spring, with all of nature coming to life, would have seemed a cruel irony; and for him to have died in the autumn would have seemed a little premature – so, somehow winter was a fitting time for him to take his leave.

Fresh snow swirled from the northern sky as they laid him to rest within the frozen prairie sod. It seems that death always brings sadness, especially under cheerless, cloudy skies. But the memory of my Uncle John, on that cold grey winter day, brought joy and inspiration as we celebrated the gift his life had been.

He had lived a rather unobtrusive life and was a man of few words. For the most part he was a farmer, but in his later years, after selling the farm, he moved into town and took up carpentry. Carpentry became for him not so much a livelihood as a spiritual vocation. I don't know what inspired him. Perhaps it was his practical and earthy identification with Jesus who was also well-acquainted with the hammer and the lathe. In any case he became a self-appointed carpenter to the widows and the poor and thrived on helping people in need. This is what warmed our hearts in remembrance of him as the snow blew cold across the frozen cemetery.

Ever since studying the plays of Shakespeare, one phrase has often come to mind when I think of the legacy of a human life, and when I ponder what might remain when the course of my own life is done. In the gripping scene following the death of Julius Caesar, Mark Antony makes an impassioned yet very callous observation that the evil that men do lives after them, but the good is oft' interred with their bones. But for my Uncle John this was not the case; it became quite the opposite. Again and again he was remembered for his selfless service and his unexpected and uncompensated work in helping people.

The good that he had done as a quiet, humble servant of Jesus Christ profoundly touched me. Consistent with St Francis's challenge in charging his fellow monks to be ready to preach the gospel at all times and in all circumstances – but to use words only when necessary – my Uncle John was a ready preacher 'par excellence.' Like an apostle bearing good news to the poor, he was at the ready both in and out of season to build what needed building and to repair what needed fixing. He was constructing the sermon of a lifetime, with the nails he used being words more eloquent and powerful than any phrases that could have been substituted for his actions. And when he lay dying, no longer able to lift a hammer or hold a nail, he whispered a short prayer for those still less fortunate than he.

My Uncle John was an apostle of the hammer and the nail. I wonder, when I'm done, what kind of apostle will I have been?

You are the light of the world. A city on a hill cannot be hidden. Neither do people light a lamp and put it under a bowl. Instead they put it on its stand, and it gives light to everyone in the house. In the same way, let your light shine before men, that they may see your good deeds and praise your Father in heaven (Matt. 5:14–16).

28

MARKETPLACE CATHEDRAL

Time seemed suspended in the splendor and the quiet of old St James Cathedral. I was overwhelmed with a feeling of awe-inspired dignity and ancient majesty as the sanctuary swallowed up my intruding presence. The blaring noise of traffic in the street and the feverish bustle of commerce melted away within another dimension of reality, a stillness suffused with an abiding sense of God's presence. As I knelt alone, I became aware of kneeling with the long lineage of people, who, through the generations, came to the cathedral seeking spiritual comfort and refuge from the everyday cares of life: generations of people who came here for consolation, celebration, and commemoration through life's passages – baptism, confirmation, marriage and death.

I felt awed by God's presence, mediated not just by the rich smells of history, soft light refracting through stained-glass windows, and the architectural majesty of soaring columns and vaulted ceilings. In the still solitude of the cathedral I sensed God's nearness, so close and real that I scarcely dared to breathe. I lingered on my knees, aware of being a tainted mortal, yet enveloped by the loving holy presence of the Lord. The clamoring thoughts of my mind and crowded preoccupations of my heart melted before Him and receded. I was kneeling in a holy place, before a holy presence – a refuge in the marketplace of my driven-ness and busyness.

Of course I know that God does not confine Himself in cathedrals, but He did seem to be far more present there than in the marketplace outside. Why is it that I consistently experience Him as being so much more accessible and real in the cathedral than in the concrete techno-sophisticated jungle of life?

Not too long ago, my attention was captivated by the idea that my living, breathing body is literally a cathedral: in the words of St Paul – 'a temple of the Holy Spirit.' While I had understood the reality of God's presence in my life through the indwelling of His Holy Spirit, I really hadn't developed a sense that my life is a cathedral literally inhabited by His presence, every bit as awe-inspiring as His presence in St James Cathedral.

Among the spiritual disciplines of classical Christian spirituality, meditation or contemplation is central. A phrase used by Brother Lawrence describes meditation as simply consisting of 'practicing the presence of Christ.' For me the conscious discipline of setting a daily time apart in order to reflect on the life of Jesus, to ponder Scripture (the Word of the Lord) and to quietly and attentively listen for the nudge of the Holy Spirit, has taken on a new significance. I have begun to understand meditation as a process through which the inner sanctuary of my life is becoming inhabited by God's presence. The cathedral of my life is being formed – a cathedral in which the peace, presence, joy, and love of the Lord is every bit as palpable and pervasive as that which I find in St James Cathedral.

Life is often consumed in frenetic activities, responsibilities and diversions. In the midst of the tumult, people often feel a gnawing spiritual hunger, a longing for spiritual refuge and connectedness. I seldom pass a cathedral without going inside, only to find the cathedral virtually deserted while the busy streets outside surge with traffic and throb with the bustle of commerce. The peace and tranquillity I tend to encounter in the cathedral does not seem to affect the tumult of the marketplace. There is such a huge gap between the reality on the street and the tranquillity in the sanctuary. As I left St James Cathedral that day and returned to the street the words of St. Paul rang in my mind with new meaning: '... you yourselves are God's temple and ... God's Spirit lives in you' (1 Cor. 3:16). You are a roving cathedral – a living cathedral in the tumult of the marketplace! Christ's presence in me took on a whole new meaning.

Will people in the marketplace and on the street find in me that reassuring peace and the presence of Christ that seems so real in the sanctuary of St. James?

For we are the temple of the living God. As God has said: 'I will live with them and walk among them, and I will be their God, and they will be my people' (2 Cor. 6:16).

29

ROAD SCHOLARS

I took pride in my deft ability to maneuver through heavy traffic during the daily rush-hour commute. Taking advantage of drivers whose split-second hesitations created openings in the flow of traffic required my total concentration. Observing and using traffic patterns to bypass slower-moving cars was an art I mastered. It was a game, and I refused to let anything or anyone impede my journey to the destination.

Then one Friday I found myself driving home through an unusual surge of weekend traffic. Mile after mile I inched along in a slow stream of vehicles numbering in the thousands if not tens of thousands. I felt trapped; there was nowhere to maneuver. My frustration grew and I was weary, hot, and very irritable.

As I crept forward in sporadic fits and starts, I noticed an old car pulled onto the shoulder of the highway. Coming alongside, I looked over to see a young woman leaning against the side of the car crying. As I passed by, her tearful face receded in my rear-view mirror. Eager to get beyond the congestion, I really did not feel like stopping to find out if she needed assistance – nobody else was stopping. Surely, with thousands of other vehicles on the road, someone else would lend a helping hand when the congestion eased. But that could be a long time.

So I reluctantly pulled onto the shoulder of the road and walked back to the car with the weeping driver. I was already delayed and I knew that stopping would delay my journey even more. Whatever the young woman's problem might be, it was undoubtedly none of my business, and there would be very little that I could do with my unfortunate mechanical abilities. As I approached her she continued to sob. She had been stranded in the roadside heat beside her broken-down vehicle for nearly two hours while an endless stream of cars were passing by. Not a single person had stopped to offer help. 'Maybe God is trying to tell me something,' she sobbed. 'I'm leaving home to move in with my boyfriend. My mother doesn't like him, and she told me it would be a big mistake. We argued, and so I just took off without even saying good-bye.'

As I gave her a ride to a mechanic's garage a few miles down the road, I asked her about God, her mother, her lover, and the destination of her life. I offered to let her use my phone to call her mother and make things right. When we reached the garage I made sure she would be okay and that was the end of that, but the experience got me thinking about the roads I travel, and how those roads are often just the means of getting from one destination to another as quickly as possible. But those roads involve more than just the interconnected destinations. Roads involve the journey, and as such they are places where we encounter other people, places where we experience and give witness of our faith.

Jesus told a story about a hapless traveler who fell prey to thieves on the road to Jericho. A stream of people saw that he was in trouble yet kept on moving, intent on reaching their destinations without interruption or incident. Brilliant scholars and devout practitioners of religious faith also saw the man but didn't stop to offer any help. They had studied enough to know the finer definitions of their faith, but all that scholarship didn't make a difference to their journey down the road.

When we are traveling toward a destination, whether on urgent business or homeward bound, it's common to treat the journey as inconsequential or secondary to the condition of the road, the volume of traffic, and ultimately to the destination. Often I have ignorantly and sometimes deliberately passed by people and situations, mistakenly believing that the destination is more important to me and to God than the journey. In actuality, though, the roads we travel are not just a means to an end – they are places where our faith is tested in the real world.

A few days after Jesus was crucified, two men walked together on the road back to Emmaus from Jerusalem. Preoccupied with the death of Jesus and subsequent reports of His unbelievable resurrection, the men were deeply engrossed in discussing the details, trying to make sense of it all. Along the way another man joined them and entered their conversation, seeming very knowledgeable. As the light of day became the dusk of evening, the men reached the village and invited the stranger to stay with them. A meal was prepared. As they broke bread together, they suddenly recognized the stranger who had accompanied them – He was the risen Jesus! While they had walked with Him and talked with Him along the dusty road, they had been so engrossed in their own concerns that they had not even recognized Him.

What would have happened if those two men had been less hospitable and hadn't invited the stranger to eat and stay with them? How often do I fail to recognize Jesus along the way because I'm too focused on my own concerns and needs and getting to my destination? How many times have I been so caught up with my own life and work that I couldn't recognize Him in people and situations along the way? So pleased to reach my destination that I simply bid farewell to the strangers I met and traveled with – and disappeared?

Jesus said He was the Way, the Truth, and the Life, and many people followed Him. Saul was intent on preserving the true religious beliefs of his people and protecting them from heretics. As a result, he was murderously intent on eliminating people

YOUR JOURNEY WITH JESUS

who believed in Jesus as the Way and the Truth. An educated man of letters, Saul was on the road to Damascus when a blinding light and a voice from heaven suddenly interrupted his travel. There in the middle of the road on his journey to Damascus he was confronted with the inadequacy of his scholarship and his wrong intentions. In that transforming encounter with Jesus, Saul became a different man – his identity, destination, and mission completely changed from his own way to the Way of Jesus.

What would have happened if Saul simply dismissed the light and voice on the road to Damascus as a hallucination – or attributed the experience to road weariness? What if he hadn't the courage to respond and alter his destination? Today it isn't through blinding light and a voice from Heaven that the Lord speaks, and interrupts the journeys of men and women. Sometimes the most poignant and dramatic encounters with Christ come by way of unexpected interruptions along the roads we travel – chance encounters with people, unexpected changes, new opportunities, obstacles and problems, and challenges and disappointments as we travel from one destination to another. While I've never encountered a blinding light or audibly heard the voice of Jesus, I do encounter the presence of Christ in the way points of the journey – in situations and people that Jesus puts into the middle of the busy road, often when I am most intent on getting to my destination.

The journey and our destination are not disconnected. I've been thinking more and more about our need to become road scholars, people of the Way of Jesus who are learning to think like Jesus, to act like Jesus, and to do the things that Jesus did as we travel from destination to destination.

Do not let your hearts be troubled. Trust in God; trust also in me. In my Father's house are many rooms; if it were not so, I would have told you. I am going there to prepare a place for you. And if I go and prepare a place for you, I will come back and take you to be with me that you also may be where I am.

You know the way to the place where I am going. Thomas said to him, 'Lord, we don't know where you are going, so how can we know the way?' Jesus answered, 'I am the way and the truth and the life' (John 14:1-6).

30

EDDIE'S SONG

Eddie Starblanket, descendent of the noble Blood Indian tribe who freely roamed the vast, expansive Canadian prairies long before the white man came.

Eddie Starblanket, descendent of a crime-plagued family, paces back and forth in the small confines of a concrete prison cell.

Eddie Starblanket, dark glasses, impassive, and remote, a solitary soul among three dozen other inmates who, out of boredom, or the desire to be freed from their six-by-eight foot cells, showed up at the weekly chapel service.

It was a typical prison chapel service of fidgeting and whispering as a hymn was sung, as prayers were offered, and as the chaplain spoke. After the final Amen it was time for tea, coffee, and conversation. It was then that Eddie came alive. He reached for a battered, old guitar, struck a lonesome chord, and began to sing. His rasping, soulful song echoed of freedom past and of a longing for freedom yet to come. Amid the ignobility of the prison, I saw the noble roots and yearning of a man who was born for freedom, not confinement. Starblanket was his name. A name handed down through generations from his ancestors who lived in freedom, blanketed only by stars above vast waves of swaying prairie grass.

I was born and raised on those same western plains that slope down from the great Canadian Rocky Mountains. Perhaps that is why, though my musical preference comprises the likes of Telemann and Vivaldi, country music continues to warm my heart like a crackling campfire on a moonlit night. Eddie's song echoed a sentiment that embodies the soul of everyday human experience, the pains and hopes of ordinary man.

As Eddie sang, the three dozen men grew quiet. Their eyes flickered with recognition. The songs resonated with the deepest yearnings of their own hearts: songs of sadness and of hope; songs of human failure and betrayal; and then the song of a Father in Heaven who cares and waits. The final song was so simple and profound it made the chaplain's words seem like a dispirited hollow echo.

Eddie Starblanket wasn't a good singer but he sang with his heart. When the final chord sank beneath the silence Eddie put down the guitar and walked away, looking only at his feet. I followed him to the coffee pot. 'That was a gospel song,' I said. 'Why sing gospel with all that other stuff?'

'Yeah,' he replied, looking at his feet, 'I am a Christian, but I'm a terrible back slider. Last time I was out I almost killed myself on drugs and whiskey. I was about dead when they found me; I think I should have died. I'd be better off.'

'God must love you very much,' I said, 'to want you alive instead of dead.'

'Nah. I don't know,' he whispered. 'In here I'm a Christian, but when I get out I always fall. There's no hope for a sinner like me.'

'But your song, Eddie, your song was about the Father who waited for his son to come back home.'

'It's no good for me, I want to, but it never works.'

'God still loves you even when you fall, Eddie, that's why you are still alive today. God did not save your life by accident.'

Eddie stopped talking as a prison officer came over to escort him back to his cell. When I left the prison a few moments later

Eddie's song was ringing in my mind. I wondered if Eddie would ever find freedom to stand again beneath that blanket of stars above the prairie night.

Eddie Starblanket, like so many others, is a man yearning for a freedom that eludes his grasp. But he knows there is a Father in Heaven with arms wide open – the same Father who put both the yearning and the song in his heart.

Eddie Starblanket – thanks for singing. Your song was a gift that touched my heart and the hearts of other prisoners. Maybe God spared your life for prison, to sing your song about the Father's love for us. He is your Father and He waits for you.

Now the tax collectors and 'sinners' were all gathering around to hear him. But the Pharisees and the teachers of the law muttered, 'This man welcomes sinners and eats with them.' Then Jesus told them this parable… 'There was a man who had two sons… [T]he younger son got together all he had, set off for a distant country and there squandered his wealth in wild living…When he came to his senses, he said… "I will set out and go back to my father."… But while he was still a long way off, his father saw him and was filled with compassion for him; he ran to his son, threw his arms around him and kissed him … [and said] "this son of mine was dead and is alive again; he was lost and is found." So they began to celebrate' (Luke 15:1-3, 11, 13, 17, 18, 20, 24).

31

THE QUESTION OF EVIL

A shocking and uncomfortable word has found its way into public discussion in the wake of global terrorism. That word is 'evil.' It is not uncommon to hear public officials speaking of terrorists and their collaborators as being evil. The very notion of evil is abhorrent and we've tended not to recognize the reality of evil in our modern world. But the idea of 'evil' has been resuscitated from the past to describe the nature of terrorism and the violent people who terrorize others.

Evil is a word that we don't use lightly in describing people. It carries with it such a finality of judgment and condemnation. The fact evil exists in the world, however, is undeniable. My involvement in the prisons of the world frequently takes me to the deepest coalface of human depravity and evil. I have been eyeball to eyeball with the degrading and destructive effects of evil in the lives of people.

The existence of evil is evidenced by criminal justice systems whose purpose is to restrain and punish those who commit acts that are not only considered harmful but evil – those who violate the public good and violate the lives of other people. By their very nature the prisons of the world are the habitation of evil-doers.

Yet most of the people I meet in prison are not much different from ordinary people on the street; they don't give off an aura of evil. Just the opposite; they seem to be surprisingly normal. Serial killers, terrorists, pedophiles, child abusers, or rapists – most of the criminals I meet do not seem to be the personification of evil. Yet there have been instances over the years when I have encountered individuals inside and outside of prison whose roiling anger and rejection of all that is good and decent literally sent chills up my spine. On more than one occasion I've had the overwhelming sense of being in the presence of evil.

Apart from such seemingly extraordinary exceptions, the idea of evil goes against the grain of postmodern thinking. The prevailing Western ethic of pluralism, tolerance, and inclusion promotes non-judgmentalism in attitudes toward people and their behavior. 'Live and let live,' we say, in the face of moral indecency and the complications of individual preferences. And when someone commits a flagrant indecency or a heinous crime, we tend to describe the person as being a psychopath, sociopath, or simply as being criminally deviant. Moreover, we analyze their behavior to look for those causes that might help us understand the person – the influence of drugs and alcohol, poverty, racism, mental incapacity, family dysfunction, social provocation, media influence, and so forth. And when such behavior is explained, we feel relieved because the cause is not evil – it is understandable.

St Thomas Aquinas described the nature of evil as the negation of being which emanates from Satan, a fallen angel whose limitations nurture a horrifying hatred of all that is good, a hatred of being itself. Historically, Christianity has defined evil as nothingness – the enemy of life. One social commentator suggested that the essence of evil is to make something into nothing, and that the climax of terrorist acts is often the willful annihilation of themselves, which is an ultimate act of allegiance to nothingness.

When God made the universe and this planet and the life that inhabits it He called it good. Satan is the antithesis of good, the great spoiler with a flaming hatred against all that God made good – nature, the environment, human life. Evil inevitably seeks to pervert, contaminate, and annihilate that which is good (truth, beauty, love, justice, faith, hope, and the like). Evil is recognized by the footprints it leaves – desolation and destruction, depravity and death, deceit and decadence.

For too long the idea of evil has been kept out of public discourse. We have been reluctant to recognize evil for what it is – the destructive force against all that is good and decent and against life itself. In our comfortable, affluent, enlightened Western cultures we've come to view evil as an archaic and almost medieval notion. Even sin is not considered as evidence of evil, but rather as simply an expression of personal preference or, at worst, weakness or failure. Thus the belief that all human behavior has cosmic implications gets lost, and the line between good and evil increasingly becomes one of a preference to be accommodated and even included.

Terrorists and suicide bombers are a wake-up call to the world, for evil has shown its face in such a way that it is recognizable and unavoidable. Yet the evil done to us is always more recognizable than is the evil we do to others. Alexander Solzhenitsyn made a frightening observation during the Soviet era when he said that 'the dividing line between good and evil does not run between east and west but through every human heart.' The dividing line between good and evil does not run between terrorists and us but through every nation, every community, and every human heart.

> Seek the LORD while he may be found;
>   call on him while he is near.
> Let the wicked forsake his way
>   and the evil man his thoughts.
> Let him turn to the LORD, and he will have mercy on him,
>   and to our God, for he will freely pardon (Isa. 55:6, 7).

32

THE FIG LEAVES OF EDEN

I wonder what I would have done had God placed me instead of Adam in the Garden of Eden. It is hard for me to imagine what it would have been like because it seems that the only limitation of freedom Adam and Eve faced was the prohibition against eating the fruit of one tree. Assuming that the Garden contained a wide diversity of plant life with all manner of other exotic fruit, what could be so difficult about abstaining from the fruit of a single tree?

Quite possibly the fruit of that tree may not have held any particular attraction by way of its exotic appearance, sensuous shape, or enticing aroma. In fact, I suspect that it may have even been unremarkable in comparison to strawberries, cherries, mangoes, papayas, kiwis, lychees, apples, oranges, and all the other wonderfully delicious fruit in the Garden. I really doubt that God would have made a tree of forbidden fruit so utterly enticing and irresistible that it completely overshadowed everything else in the Garden. Yet the fruit of the tree did attract peculiar attraction simply because it was singled out as the only thing off limits, the only thing God held back from the very people He had made in His own image. And so when the day came when Adam and Eve stopped naked before that tree and looked up at its luscious fruit, it became attractive to them in spite of all the other wonderful fruit in the Garden. It was the only fruit standing between them and God.

I'd like to think that I would not have been so quick to eat of the fruit and that I could have avoided the tree altogether. What could possibly be so special about just one tree? How difficult could it be to live denying oneself the taste of just a single kind of fruit? And yet, why would God prohibit me from picking the fruit of just one tree when He has already given me full reign and responsibility for everything else in the Garden? Obviously I am not as free as I thought I was; I am but one tree removed from full control. Since God gave me authority and responsibility over absolutely everything except for one tree, the Garden is obviously mine. It is my place, my property, my decision! Why on earth should God deny me anything? I am entitled – it's mine, it's mine, it's mine!

As these thoughts creep into my consciousness, I begin to realize just why that measly little fruit tree seems so attractive. Only by plucking its fruit will I be able to assert my absolute dominance and God-denied freedom. Why not?

I cannot imagine what the fruit might have tasted like, but I suspect it had a bittersweet flavor – perhaps more bitter than sweet, like an unexpectedly sour cherry. But suddenly it's too late for the deed is done. The fruit, bitter and uneaten, drops from my hand as fear rips through the core of my being. My deliberate assertion of freedom, power, and control over my life and world is darkened by the sudden realization that I'm standing naked and exposed in front of God's tree in the middle of the Garden. It's His only tree – all the rest were mine! I run and try to hide myself in the camouflage of fig leaves, anything to cover up my deed, to disguise the reality of myself in the recesses of the Garden.

The story of the Garden of Eden is in a real sense my own story as it is the story of each of us, for none of us really fare much better than Adam did. We have a tendency to become fixated on the forbidden fruit; we desire nothing more and nothing less than to totally please ourselves, to do our own thing, to do it our way, to be the masters of our own destiny. Slowly we come to realize, often painfully, that so much of our lives and so many of our decisions are tainted by selfishness and pride. Like Adam, our actions are rooted in the impulse to stand against God Himself, to be the sovereign lords of our own lives, to have things our way. It may not be in ways as singular and pivotal as plucking the forbidden fruit and taking a big bite of it, but our propensity as human beings is one of naked pride and an inclination to camouflage our very nakedness with fig leaves of rationality, respectability, magnanimity, and even religion.

But when God walks into the Garden there is no place to hide, no camouflage to disguise reality. Yet this same God who placed us in the Garden, whose tree we violated and violate, loves us with immeasurable grace and mercy. It is He who, with arms extended, hangs naked and exposed on the tree of shame in our place and for our sake. Our nakedness is exchanged for His, and as He turned to the naked thief on the cross, He also turns to us to invite us back to the Paradise we violated, and to intimate friendship with Him.

Then the angel showed me the river of the water of life, as clear as crystal, flowing from the throne of God and of the Lamb down the middle of the great street of the city. On each side of the river stood the tree of life, bearing twelve crops of fruit, yielding its fruit every month. And the leaves of the tree are for the healing of the nations. No longer will there be any curse. The throne of God and of the Lamb will be in the city, and his servants will serve him. They will see his face, and his name will be on their foreheads. There will be no more night. They will not need the light of a lamp or the light of the sun, for the Lord God will give them light. And they will reign for ever and ever (Rev. 22:1-5).

33

HANDS OF HATRED

Hatred is not a pretty sight. It is not just hatred broiling between adversaries that is ugly. Uglier by far is hatred unleashed against those who are defenseless and marginalized, and even hatred that vents itself against animals – defenseless creatures that cannot compete with or insult human beings.

My wife has a very tender heart toward animals and supports several animal protection and rescue organizations. One day as I was paging through one of the many periodicals she receives I was shocked by photo after photo of dogs, horses, cats, and other animals that have been rescued from the sadistic and destructive hands of abusive owners. The sight of battered, bruised, and beaten animals was gruesome. My heart went out to those creatures and I thanked God for people of good intentions who rescue and care for them.

Even though we have adopted two unwanted dogs through our local animal rescue league, I have always been more preoccupied with and concerned about the condition and needs of human beings who suffer brutality and hatred at the hands of other human beings. Yet as I paged through the magazine I was appalled by the senseless hatred expressed through human hands.

I looked down at my own hands and wondered if they are capable of expressing such hatred. My fists are not clenched in anger and they bear no stains of violence – my hands are clean!

I gazed upon my open hands with a growing sense of satisfied pride and began thinking about the many men, women, and young people I have met in the prisons of the world whose hands are calloused and bloodstained with hatred. My thoughts turned to hatred close at hand: a teenager who shot himself because he hated his family and his own life; a respected and successful businessman who beat his wife senseless in a drunken terror; an awkward young man who deliberately set fire to a neighbor's house and then the parish church; a father who, for years, forced his two young daughters to satisfy his perverse sexual urges – people whose hands touch the world with hatred.

Hateful hands are those which destroy families, communities, societies, and the created world around us. A recent newscast covering the political and social turmoil in the Middle East graphically depicted a crowd of thousands with clenched fists upraised in hateful protest against their adversary. And when our own eyes focus on the illogical and venomous hatred brewing between certain countries some of us also raise our hands in anger and disgust (or is it also hatred?) against those people and the perversity of their leaders.

I looked away from my own hands realizing that, while my fist is not upraised in hatred and while my hands are not stained with violence, I am not a man without hate. For hatred does not begin in the palm of one's hands; it begins in the heart. How often my own impatience, irritability, anger, argumentativeness, and frustration have kindled a small fire in my heart that begins throwing up sparks of hate. In *Macbeth* Shakespeare graphically portrays hatred as being not about bloodstained hands but about the nature of the heart. After Macbeth has been murdered, Lady Macbeth is obsessed with making sure that her hands are washed and clean, yet as much as she washes she cannot rid herself of guilt for the hatred that has taken root in her heart and contributed to the murder of Macbeth. Like Lady Macbeth or Pilate at the trial of Jesus, the stains of hatred and responsibility cannot be removed by the washing of one's hands.

On several occasions I have traveled to Medellin, Colombia, home to international drug cartels and notorious for its pervasive violence. During dinner one evening I met a young ex-prisoner who had been involved with one of the cartels both as a coca producer and as an 'enforcer.' He was a man whose hands bore all of the stains of a hate-filled lifestyle. While serving time in prison he encountered the love and mercy of Jesus Christ for the first time. It radically transformed his life. His passions turned from crime and violence to peace and love. While completing his prison sentence he became a very gifted wood carver and when he was released he became a professional artisan. While his hands could never begin to undo the hate, damage, and destruction they had caused, they now turned to creativity as he praised the Lord through his art. As he told me the story of his life he raised his calloused hands into the air and said, 'These hands that once did hateful things are now the hands that praise the Lord – the bloodstains on His hands have set mine free.'

> No good tree bears bad fruit, nor does a bad tree bear good fruit. Each tree is recognized by its own fruit. People do not pick figs from thornbushes, or grapes from briers. The good man brings good things out of the good stored up in his heart, and the evil man brings evil things out of the evil stored up in his heart. For out of the overflow of his heart his mouth speaks (Luke 6:43-45).

34

By God's Finger

On the ceiling of the Sistine Chapel in Rome, a magnificent series of paintings depicts the biblical story of creation. Originally painted by Michelangelo 500 years ago, these recently restored paintings are astonishing in their provocative vitality and grandeur. The scene of God creating the sun, moon, and plants depicts Him in mid-crouch, leaping through the clouds, arms outstretched, as the majesty of the whole universe springs into being from the tip of His extended forefingers. The painting is charged with the exuberant drama of God creating life.

The most poignant scene in the series is the creation of Adam. Michelangelo portrays God stretching forth His right hand from heaven, forefinger reaching down toward Adam, who is a perfectly formed figure languidly crouching on the ground. Adam appears as if he is awakening from slumber but not yet alive. His arm is partly raised, and his hand reaches toward the outstretched hand of God. Yet they don't quite touch; there is a space between them. The painting is poised in suspense and expectation, focused on the poignant synapse separating God's outstretched finger and the languid hand of Adam. God is on the verge of creating something unexpected and profound, man alive! By the touch of God's finger Adam is about to become the likeness of God's own image!

As I contemplated the paintings, I found myself totally gripped by the image of God's finger. By the finger of God, the entire universe was flung into created motion. Stars sparkled across the heavenly expanse; flowers carpeted high meadows in a dazzling array of color and scintillating scent; bird-songs trilled through deep forests and across far-flung fields; and all manner of exotic beasts began propagating their own kind. And finally, by the touch of God's finger, a solitary man breathed life and got up from the dust to reflect the divine image of his Maker. By God's finger, everything was made from nothing; by His finger, reality became fashioned from the unimaginable; by His finger, beauty blossomed from the fathomless void; and by His finger, life was born from the common dust of the ground.

Yet as I contemplated the painting I could not help but think about the space between God's outstretched finger and Adam's languid uplifted hand. It seemed to me that this is the same space where I live most of my life – a space waiting for God to act, waiting for His touch. It is a space not just of expectation and longing, but often an empty space of awareness, asleep to the creative presence and power of God. God has created, God has acted, and I inhabit a space that is occasionally filled with the electrifying sense of His presence – but more often it is a waiting, wanting void. Yet it is in only in this space that I can experience the touch of the God of all creation – the touch of life and of vitality that I cannot give myself.

More than three thousand years ago, an extraordinary group of court magicians came to the end of their science when they discovered that they were no match against the finger of God. As they saw it, the 'finger of God' (Exod. 8:19) was responsible for the disasters that were falling upon them, threatening their livelihood. There was no other explanation – and there was nothing they could do. In their nation, the most powerful nation in the world, the illusions of ultimate power and control were being undone. Neither their best magic nor the cutting edge of their science could replicate or counter the 'natural' calamities coming against them by the simple word of a man who claimed to speak for God – 'let my people go!'

By the finger of God, the most powerful leaders of that most powerful nation had no option but to relinquish control to the God of a powerless, oppressed people who had been denied the freedom they could never win on their own.

Then, as now, people often recognize the intervention of God, but when His finger is withdrawn, they return to the illusions and delusions of their own making. With the corpses of their first-born sons barely in the grave, those powerful Egyptian oppressors mounted a military counterattack to recapture their God-emancipated slaves. For them it was an economic necessity; the sustainability of their way of life totally depended on it. But God was not yet finished.

And not too long after that, the miraculously freed ragtag nation of liberated slaves, with the memory of God's miraculous rescue ebbing from their minds, wearied as they waited for their leader to bring God's word to them from the mountain-top. So they decided to create their own deity, fashioning him as a golden glistening bull of their own creative imagination.

More than a thousand years later, God chose to visit those liberated people who had once again become subject to a foreign power. Through Jesus God tangibly demonstrated His enduring compassion for groveling beggars, lonely widows, arrogant sinners, and suffering victims. God reached out his finger to heal unsightly lepers and crippled limbs; He beckoned the dead back to life and pointedly ordered demons out of the oppressed. Yet Jesus was constantly barraged with questions and criticism from those who closed their eyes and steeled their hearts against the things that only God could do among them.

In response to criticism by a particular group of religious leaders, Jesus challenged them to see that He was acting 'by the finger of God' (Luke 11:20). On yet another occasion, when a group of people attempted to trap Him in a moral judgment based on their own terms, He stooped before them and 'with his finger' (John 8:6) inscribed mercy on the dust beneath their feet and beneath their dignity. In sullen silence they saw the finger of God write forgiveness, but in prideful anger they left the scene to plot revenge.

By the finger of God, the universe and everything in it was brought into being. By the finger of God, human life was endowed with His own image. By the finger of God, people in bondage were led from captivity to freedom. By the finger of God, ordinary and extraordinary blessings demonstrated His grace and mercy among suffering human beings. By the finger of God, His love and presence continue to be written in the dust of our lives and inscribed on our stony hearts.

But there is a space between God's finger and our lives. It is a space where faith encounters grace, where those with ears to hear begin to understand, and where those with eyes to see begin to discern the presence of the Lord of all creation.

But if I drive out demons by the finger of God, then the kingdom of God has come to you (Luke 11:20).

35

IN THIS SIGN CONQUER!

The Roman Empire was disarrayed, fragmented, and sharply divided. With six powerful 'Caesars' and their armies vying for supremacy, the powerful world-dominating Roman Empire was being destroyed from the inside out. On a much larger scale it was, perhaps, not unlike the bloody disintegration of countries today when central authority loses its mandate, when political and military forces polarize the country, and lifelong neighbors become enemies of one another.

This was the political and social scene when Constantine, a brilliant Roman general and military strategist, seized initiative in the midst of the Empire's impending political and economic disaster. Through a series of successful battles, he quickly overpowered his nearest rivals, and then advanced on Rome to confront his greatest opponent, emperor Maxentius.

The two armies confronted each other in what would be a fight to the finish at Milvian Bridge on the Tiber River. On the eve of battle, facing the most crucial military engagement of his life, a sign in the heavens shattered Constantine's concentration on the coming battle. Although he was not a believer, what he saw was a cross with an inscription saying, 'In this sign conquer.'

Drawing moral courage and confidence from this momentous revelation, Constantine spurred his forces into battle and overwhelmingly routed the army of Maxentius. Constantine went on to become the undisputed emperor, saving the Roman Empire from disintegration.

While we do not know whether Constantine's vision on the eve of battle was really a God-given sign, we know that it gave him the courage and determination to prevail in the coming battle. When the battle was finally won, he unequivocally attributed his victory to the sign of the cross. Emerging from the battle at Milvian Bridge, the cross was raised to become the symbol, not of the beleaguered and suffering followers of Jesus but of the powerful 'Holy' Roman Empire. Emblazoned on military arsenals and on the edicts of government, the cross came to signify the 'divine' might and right of the Empire itself.

During the 300 years preceding the ascent of Constantine, followers of Jesus identified the cross with suffering, sacrifice, and even martyrdom. It was the cross on which Jesus submitted to insult, humiliation, and torture – giving up His own life to save the world. The cross was at the heart of their faith in Jesus – God crucified and rising again, God's scandalous love in the redemptive sacrifice of Jesus Christ. The cross was anything but a symbol of human might and power prevailing over evil.

Constantine's victory at Milvian Bridge and his adoption of the cross as the symbol of the Empire changed the holy meaning of that symbol. The cross, now planted in the public square by the authority of the state, increasingly became a symbol of human power. The way of the cross, of self-giving love and sacrifice for others, became overshadowed by the way of the state.

While those who followed Jesus knew that His sacrificial suffering on the cross was a spiritual triumph of love over evil, they gradually became seduced by the unprecedented peace, privilege, and power afforded by the Empire. No longer was the cross a scandal; it was normalized and legitimized as the official mark of power, the symbol of the Roman Empire.

Under Constantine, the church, having survived three centuries of persecution and harassment, entered a new era of acceptability and influence. The church flourished, spreading to every province of the Empire. The amalgamation of the Empire and the cross had significantly helped in spreading the gospel and establishing the church. Yet even as the church flourished under the protection and assistance of the Empire she began to lose the essence of 'the way of the cross.' The humble self-giving and sacrificial way of love was overtaken by the easier way of influence and power.

We see the same tendency today in our own lives to avoid or to be drawn away from the humble, self-giving way of the cross. How much easier it is to assert power or impose our cross of influence in the moral and political 'culture wars' of our times. But I wonder if the way of power is the true way of doing the gospel – might we too be turning our backs on the sacrificial way of the cross, the way of love by which the real victory over evil was won by Jesus? What is the way of the cross for those of us who live in a religion-tolerant society? Is the cross only a historical symbol of the spiritual heart of our faith? Or is the cross the symbol of a way of life that puts selflessness and sacrificial love for others, even enemies, above the use of imposing our will and way over others?

It continues to amaze me that, while I was still an unbeliever – an 'enemy of the cross' – Jesus loved me so much that He suffered on that cross to give up His own life for me. It was through His suffering love and amazing grace that my heart was touched, in a way that it would not have been touched through an imposition of power or a force of argument.

In my world of criminal justice today there is a tendency to think that the crime crisis can be overcome through political resolve, tough laws, and swifter more punitive justice – by controlling evil-doers, degraders of decency, and subverters of truth by means of force and power. It does not work! But I've seen tough, incorrigible offenders change through love, through relationships with people who care enough to suffer with them, to be compassionate, tender, truthful, and forgiving. And in my own life, I know that when I take the difficult way of loving instead of lording it over others, the true power of the cross emerges.

In this sign we conquer – the self-giving way of the cross on which our Savior humbled Himself and loved us to death.

... Christ crucified: a stumbling block to Jews and foolishness to Gentiles, but to those whom God has called, both Jews and Greeks, Christ the power of God and the wisdom of God. For the foolishness of God is wiser than man's wisdom, and the weakness of God is stronger than man's strength (1 Cor. 1:23-25).

If anyone would come after me, he must deny himself and take up his cross daily and follow me. For whoever wants to save his life will lose it, but whoever loses his life for me will save it (Luke 9:23, 24).

36

A TALE OF TWO MONUMENTS

'It was the best of times, it was the worst of times...' Thus begins Charles Dickens's *A Tale of Two Cities*. In the midst of the social turmoil during the French Revolution he paints a vivid picture of the suffering and anguish of the peasants and poor in contrast to the pretentious consumption of the wealthy upper class. The dichotomy portrayed in Dickens's story of the eighteenth century is still a painful reality in much of the world.

For many years I have been commuting between the consumption and frivolity of wealthy nations preoccupied with the productivity of their economies and the politics of power, and the sobering reality of nations where people are preoccupied with day-to-day survival under the appalling stench of death. The contrast between the privileged elite and the suffering masses of the world is an acid eating at the soul of our times.

We don't have to go very far out of our way to see this. In Washington D.C., seat of the world's current superpower, the contrast could not be more dramatic. A short distance from the stately White House and Capitol Buildings, with their beautifully manicured and well-protected grounds, one finds the crumbling neighborhoods of the poor and unemployed. These are crime-ridden streets, in the shadow of the White House, where suffering and violence are as palpable as the contrasting power and prestige just a few blocks away. Does it have to be this way?

One of the oldest prisons in Australia was built during the colonial period and is a typical fortress-like institution in the style of Her Majesty's penitentiaries. On a visit some years ago, I found the huge overpopulated prison still in use even though there were no toilet and sanitation facilities in any of the cells. The prisoners had to use communal 'slop' buckets in their cells. Various government studies had called for the renovation of the prison and the installation of proper plumbing in order to reduce the risk of disease and to make the environment less demeaning. The proposed renovations, however, were opposed by the local historical society who had declared the prison to be a historical monument. As a consequence, renovations to the prison were prohibited as these would detract from the historic value of the building. And so the community preservation of a building for historical purposes became more important than the dignity and needs of the men from the community who were imprisoned within. While elitist historical societies sipped wine from crystal goblets the prisoners continued to carry stinking buckets of raw sewage from their cells.

In India I came across a historic church that might as well be called a prison. It is a grand old church situated in a spacious garden amid the hubbub of a congested city. The church was founded by one of the great missionaries to India who planted it in the heart of the seamy side of town in order to reach out to dock workers, transient sailors, prostitutes, and the ever-present beggars and orphans on the street.

It soon became one the great mission churches of the world and today still stands where it was founded, an edifice adorned with a bright sign proclaiming 'Jesus Saves.' But the church has become a monument, a protected island, isolated from the teeming surge of needy street people and beggars with a huge wrought-iron fence to keep the grounds and building safe and the congregation from being harassed. And so the preservation of another building becomes more valuable than the preservation of a vision to reach out to the broken and emaciated lives of people. Now the affluent congregation listens to learned men preach while the elderly, sick, and infant children die on the pain-smeared streets.

It is the best of times, it is the worst of times – but for good times and bad times, for rich and poor, imprisoned and free, saint and sinner, the only real good news is that Jesus Christ gave Himself to save people, not to preserve monuments. Yet we are so easily inclined to preserve our gains, our assets, our success, our freedom and our blessings – turning them into monuments instead of expending them where God's compassion lives.

Monuments don't live!

The ground of a certain rich man produced a good crop. He thought to himself, 'What shall I do? I have no place to store my crops.' Then he said, 'This is what I'll do. I will tear down my barns and build bigger ones, and there I will store all my grain and my goods. And I'll say to myself, "You have plenty of good things laid up for many years. Take life easy; eat, drink and be merry."' But God said to him, 'You fool! This very night your life will be demanded from you. Then who will get what you have prepared for yourself?' This is how it will be with anyone who stores up things for himself but is not rich toward God (Luke 12:16-21).

37

In the Proper Season

The huge Dutch-colonial prison was a warehouse of misery. I could see that, in spite of the flowers lining the walkway leading to the prison chapel. We were already late, but as we hurried past the gloomy cell-blocks I peered into their seemingly endless corridors of grimy grey and steel. I could almost taste the foul stale air of human degradation and despair.

We turned a corner entering a gateway that opened into a small walled courtyard surrounding a chapel. It was a pleasant place by very basic standards, and was obviously a place of rare respite from monotonous prison life. The chapel was packed to capacity. Today was a special day and more than the usual number of inmates had turned out to meet the foreign guests.

But we had been delayed and now it was almost noon. I got the feeling, on entering the chapel, of a party that had already been delayed too long. Prisoners were packed together on close rows of backless benches and apart from a wheezing fan near the altar there was no relief from the steaming air of the tropical rainy season. It was obvious to me that we had run out of both time and tolerance, so when the leader of the meeting asked me to simply bring official greetings from Prison Fellowship International, I was only too eager to comply.

The greetings I began delivering were from their brothers and sisters in prisons around the world – in Africa, America, Latin America, Europe, and Asia. Even as I spoke the words I sensed the utter cosmic futility of those very greetings. The eyes of the prisoners reflected interest, but in the depths of their expressions I became aware of a deeper need – something that would never be touched by greetings and tokens of human solidarity alone. Furthermore, I hadn't traveled the more than 9,000 miles just to come here as an international courier of good will and good words. It dawned on me more powerfully than ever before that my sole purpose for being there was Christ – as His ambassador.

Immediately, I continued, 'But I haven't come here just to bring you news from your brothers and sisters around the world, fellow prisoners; I've come here because of a prisoner who changed my life. I've come here because of Jesus Christ, who is the only one who fully understands your pain and circumstances, and who is the only one who takes His place with us in the midst of life's deepest misery.' I was compelled to go beyond the greetings to tell them about Jesus Christ who was a prisoner even through the agonizing wait for execution on false charges and after an unfair trial.

Shortly thereafter the meeting ended, following which the men lingered to shake hands (more than two hundred sweaty palms). About half of them were Muslims, which I hadn't realized, and so that alone made me glad that I had responded to the prompting of the Holy Spirit to speak of Jesus. A number of the men were also political prisoners under sentence of death; some had been languishing in prison for twenty years not knowing from one day to the next if it might be their last.

The following day I was at yet another old colonial prison in a different city and again our group was running late. This prison wasn't even on our schedule, but when someone heard that it would be possible for us to meet with some of the inmates it was decided that we should not pass up the opportunity. We walked through the towering wall and steel gates towards the chapel even as the call to evening prayers was issuing from the minaret of the prison mosque. By contrast the Christian chapel was empty and silent when we entered. Its cavernous space hearkened back to a time when the colonial rulers mandated the attendance of all prisoners in Christian worship. Nowadays, though, the mosque was the center of religious life, while the old Christian chapel with its crumbling stations of the cross had become a virtually empty relic, save for two short rows of seats and an altar that served a handful of Christian prisoners.

Time was getting really short by now and my hosts, as they had done the previous day, again entreated me to bring only greetings because we were going to be late for another meeting in a nearby town. Slowly a dozen inmates straggled into the chapel and we introduced ourselves. This time I knew for certain the purpose for which I had come. Time was short but so important that, regardless of the pressing schedule, it was the appointed time to talk to the men about Jesus Christ, their fellow prisoner.

Later that evening, as the meeting in town was drawing to a close, word of bad news came to us from the capital city – from the prison we had visited the day before. Four men were executed by firing squad that morning: four men who had been waiting twenty years for the dreaded day of execution. Without warning that day arrived, the morning after I visited three of those men in prison. Disbelief and pain seared through me as I listened to the news – what if yesterday I had stood before those men on the brink of their eternity only to bring greetings from other prisoners in other places! What a waste of time and effort that would have been, what squander of a holy trust.

There can only be one reason why any of us who follow Jesus Christ do what we do in life. Everything that we do is a witness, a ministry of nudging people toward an encounter with the truth, love, and mercy of Jesus Christ – in season and out of season, it is the proper time.

In the presence of God and of Christ Jesus, who will judge the living and the dead, and in view of his appearing and his kingdom, I give you this charge: Preach the Word; be prepared in season and out of season; correct, rebuke and encourage – with great patience and careful instruction... [K]eep your head in all situations, endure hardship, do the work of an evangelist, discharge all the duties of your ministry (2 Tim. 4:1-2, 5).

38

BLESSED BY THE POOR

We found her living on a precariously steep hillside just outside of San Salvador. Like most of her neighbors, she had lost almost everything she owned to the devastating earthquakes that shook El Salvador that year. When the earth heaved and the mountainside shifted, her flimsy one-room shack collapsed and slid into the muddy ravine below. Yet Marie Luz and her three young daughters survived unscathed.

Marie Luz is a prison visitor and she lives up to her name – 'Luz' – 'light,' Mary of the Light. One would expect that a woman who has suffered as much as she has might be more preoccupied with her own survival than with the needs of others. But this was not the case with Marie Luz. Widowed several years ago, she was left to fend for herself and three young daughters. Illiterate and unskilled, she picked up odd jobs in the city barely managing to keep her family fed and clothed. But when the earthquakes caused her house to collapse, what little she owned was completely destroyed or salvaged and stolen by other people – like the little kerosene burner that served as her stove.

In spite of the tragedy everyone who knew Mari Luz considered her to be one of the most joyful, caring, and generous prison visitors. I wanted to see for myself. As we drove laboriously up the steep rocky trail toward the ruined shanties on the mountainside, the ruin and devastation of the earthquake was clearly visible. But nothing prepared me for the devastation we found where Marie Luz lived. Somehow she had managed to salvage parts of the collapsed walls and to find enough scraps of plastic and tin to fashion a makeshift roof. A tattered cloth covered the broken doorway. Inside, little remained of what little she had before the quake. A small, torn, and dirt-stained mattress was the only piece of 'furniture,' and during the night Marie Luz would sleep on the dirt floor so that her three daughters could have the mattress.

I've encountered poverty and witnessed the aftermath of disaster in many parts of the world. The poor always seem to be the double victims when disaster strikes. So I was amazed when we met Marie Luz. She came running down the rocky trail to meet us, a smile on her face and arms outstretched welcoming us to her home. In contrast to the abject conditions on that hillside, her eyes sparkled with joy and life. I could hardly comprehend the love that emanated from such a frail-looking woman. She exuded such a joyful inner peace, an infectious testimony of her faith.

Marie Luz told us that she considers herself a privileged servant of the Lord. 'Privileged?' I thought as she talked about her visits to the prisoners. 'Why do you even care about the prisoners?' I asked her. A smile crossed her face. Wordlessly she pointed a calloused finger to the sky. 'It's because Jesus loves me,' she said. 'The prisoners are much worse off than I am; they need love too.' It didn't take me long to discover that her love was sacrificial. Before and even after the earthquake ruined her home Marie Luz made the difficult trip into the city to collect food from the people she knows. The food was not for herself, even though her own plate was often very meager; the food was lovingly prepared to feed sick and hungry prisoners.

As we looked at the ruins of her home and saw the vulnerability of her precarious plot of land to landslides and to flooding, we suggested that she should relocate to another place. But Marie Luz was quick to object, 'This is home and these are my people – I care about them and cannot leave them.'

Some of the most remarkable people I have met around the world are not presidents or judges, government leaders or church officials, or wealthy generous entrepreneurs – the most outstanding people I have met are poor like Marie Luz. Again and again my compassion and love for others seems so paltry in comparison to people like Marie Luz who gives so joyfully and freely out of their need. Like her they don't give their 'sacrifice' a second thought; it is a natural expression of their love for Christ and their love for others. I am blessed by the poor – for the poor are blessed people to whom the Kingdom of Heaven is being given.

The brother in humble circumstances ought to take pride in his high position. But the one who is rich should take pride in his low position, because he will pass away like a wild flower. For the sun rises with scorching heat and withers the plant; its blossom falls and its beauty is destroyed. In the same way, the rich man will fade away even while he goes about his business. Blessed is the man who perseveres under trial, because when he has stood the test, he will receive the crown of life that God has promised to those who love him (James 1:9-12).

39

DIPLOMACY AND THE GOSPEL

I don't like being misunderstood or misinterpreted. For that reason I am not one of those people who boldly shares his faith with every seat-mate on the plane or train. I want to get to know people and where people are coming from so I can speak of my faith in the context of their lives. I suppose one of the reasons for this is that I don't want to be dismissed as an ancient and unthinking Bible thumper, or a raving religious fanatic, or worse yet as a narrow-minded fundamentalist. I want to be able to articulate and give account of my faith in a language and style that connects with people.

Increasingly I find that we live and work in a context that is becoming more and more pluralistic. The world is changing and even as tolerance and inclusion become the bywords of our culture there is less and less public tolerance for Christian, moral, and spiritual convictions. A great deal of sensitivity and understanding are needed for people who desire to communicate their faith in a way that connects with other people. It isn't easy, and my experience is littered with the unwitting mistakes of failed communications and misunderstandings.

Most of my life's work has been in countries other than my own. Early on I learned the value of studying the culture, geography, customs, and even the language of other countries. I was amazed how much easier it was to build relationships and to communicate with other people when I knew something about their lives and could connect with important elements of their culture. If there is an essential skill required in communicating the message of the gospel it is diplomacy – the art of learning how to speak the truth of one culture into that of another. That's what diplomats and ambassadors do, for they are essentially resident aliens who owe their allegiance to another country and represent the interests of that country in a foreign land.

When I go into prison I think of myself as a diplomat of the gospel. Prison is also a very different world, often with its own language and its own culture. When I first began going to prison I went in literally as an alien, without understanding or caring about the prison culture, and speaking in an alien language that did not connect with life as it is in prison. It was a disaster. Gradually, however, as I took an interest in prisoners and their world I developed an understanding and empathy for what it means to be imprisoned – rejected by society, labeled 'bad,' separated from family, powerless and humiliated. Over time I learned to speak in a manner and in a language that touches the heart of prison reality.

Gospel diplomacy requires patience and sensitivity, the ability to study, observe, and relate to the nuances of what people say and how they respond to what is being said. As Christ's ambassadors we work as aliens on foreign soil in contexts that are sometimes hostile to the gospel. As diplomats we face two main dangers in our communication. On the one hand we may tend to be so constrained by our own language terminology and concepts that when we speak we speak as foreigners who are unintelligible to other people. We come across as aliens with an unintelligible message and an incomprehensible mindset. This represents our failure to translate our message into language and terminology, and concepts or ideas, which people can relate to. I've seen this happen when people go into prison to preach a churchy message to hungry, lonely inmates but their message is so churchy in style and language that it doesn't connect with the gritty, sordid reality of imprisonment.

On the other hand we may put such an undue emphasis on relevance that the message is so watered down it offers no truth that is different from the familiar world-view of the culture. The message is lost. And I have also seen this happen in prison when people coming in from outside are so ill at ease and have such a personal need to identify with the inmates that they adopt and mimic the language and the manner of prisoners in order to be like them. They become a caricature because it isn't real and the message isn't heard.

A vivid example of the challenge we face as diplomats of the gospel comes from India, where one of the great challenges facing Christians is to communicate the reality of Jesus Christ in such a way that He isn't totally unintelligible to the Hindu mind. At the same time the message of the gospel can very easily be reduced to such common ideas and terms that the reality of Jesus Christ is incorporated into the common belief system of reincarnation and the multiplicity of gods. So what if God became incarnated as a man, so what if Jesus Christ is God – just another god among many other gods. No harm, no significance in that! So how does one communicate Christ in a way that can be understood? Did Mother Teresa do that on the streets of Calcutta when she embraced the dying poor with the love of Jesus?

As diplomats we must be sensitive and skillful in projecting the Christian message and our mission in such a way as both to build understanding and to challenge the prevailing perspectives of people. If we speak and act only as aliens, our message will be unintelligible. If we reduce our message and our way of living into only being culturally relevant, it will cease to challenge the prevailing world-view. A skillful diplomat builds understanding without diffusing or losing the essence of his message.

Diplomats of the gospel must present themselves and their message to their world in a way that connects to other people, yet without sacrificing the content of the message for the sake of personal acceptance or distorting it for relevance. That's what I think Paul did when he faced a meeting of the Areopagus.

> A group of Epicurean and Stoic philosophers began to dispute with him [Paul]. Some of them asked, 'What is this babbler trying to say?' Others remarked, 'He seems to be advocating foreign gods.' They said this because Paul was preaching the good news about Jesus and the resurrection. Then they took him and brought him to a meeting of the Areopagus, where they said to him, 'May we know what this new teaching is that you are presenting? You are bringing some strange ideas to our ears, and we want to know what they mean.' ... Paul then stood up in the meeting of the Areopagus and said: 'Men of Athens! I see that in every way you are very religious. For as I walked around and looked carefully at your objects of worship, I even found an altar with this inscription: TO AN UNKNOWN GOD. Now what you worship as something unknown I am going to proclaim to you (Acts 17:18-20, 22-23).

40

THE WORD OF THE LORD!

'[T]he word of the LORD came to me' (Ezek. 3:16). I stumbled somewhat uncomfortably across this simple phrase in the biblical account of Ezekiel. How could it be that Ezekiel could actually hear the word of the Lord while most of the time I only seem able to read about it, or read the words that were spoken by the Lord a long time ago. 'Again the word of the LORD came to me,' writes Ezekiel (22:23). I wonder why he could hear the word of the Lord so often and the space around me is filled only with the sounds of silence. Am I so terribly deaf that I couldn't hear the Lord even if He were to speak? Is there something so wrong with me that the Lord doesn't want to speak to me very often? Am I listening for the wrong kind of voice or sound? These questions raced through my mind as I pondered the story of Ezekiel.

Suddenly, the jangling ring of the telephone interrupted my silent thoughts. I turned away from Ezekiel and entered into a conversation that was far too long and unnecessary. It was mostly a one-way conversation that was more than I had patience to endure and I managed to bring it to a close. So many words from one person! Why does it sometimes seem that the world is full of so many people of so many words? But where is the word of the Lord when I need it?

I turned back into the sacred space of empty silence, the record of Ezekiel's encounters with the Lord still before me. The entire book of Ezekiel seemed to resonate with the vibrant life of a man in close communication with God. By contrast to the sacred silence of my book-filled library God routinely broke through the sacred silence to speak directly with Ezekiel.

As the silence became unbearable I had the urge to leave the library and go for a long run through the woods. Often when I feel dull and uninspired I go running to clear my mind and to reinvigorate myself. Most of the time I find these running respites to be exhilarating, but occasionally I feel like I am only plodding along sluggishly and am completely unable to transcend the thoughts that are bothering me. So it was one of those sluggish plodding days, and I began to wish I'd never started.

When I finally reached the end of my circuit I checked my watch and was surprised to see that I had run the five-mile course in exactly the time as the previous day when I had felt far more energized and agile. I realized that my running time had little to do with how I felt. All of a sudden, the word of the Lord seemed to come to me as a whisper in the silence – 'running has more to do with discipline and determination than with mood and feeling.' In that small moment I realized that the word of the Lord is not just a sound but that it is a holy presence in the silence, a nudging of the Holy Spirit, the remembrance of a written word, and fellowship with the incarnate Word – Jesus.

What holds true in my running is also true in my Christian walk. Certainly, there are times when I experience the word of the Lord breaking through the silence, inspiring and motivating me to keep moving forward, no matter what. But most of the time my walk of faith feels very routine and ordinary, and it takes sheer determination and discipline just to keep moving.

I long to hear the clear word of the Lord more often like Ezekiel did. Yet most of life is lived not on the high peaks of inspiration but on the vast plateaus of daily routine and responsibility. It's easy to hear the word of the Lord when it comes to us on the peaks of exhilarating spiritual encounter. But, in truth, that doesn't happen everyday. God is the One who comes to us not only in word but in the silence of our lives.

Usually when I spend time with men and women in prison I try to assure them that they are not forgotten or abandoned by God their Heavenly Father. He has not turned His face the other way or hidden Himself in the cathedral or the church. God is present in the despair, decay, and dullness of the prison – and he speaks, 'I love you, I am with you always.'

Sometimes we are prisoners too – prisoners of responsibility and the routine expectations of life. When God seems not to speak to you take heart, be of good courage, and keep moving forward, for God is present in the silence – and in the hubbub too.

> The LORD is my shepherd, I shall not be in want.
>> He makes me lie down in green pastures,
> he leads me beside quiet waters,
>> he restores my soul.
> He guides me in paths of righteousness
>> for his name's sake.
> Even though I walk
>> through the valley of the shadow of death,
> I will fear no evil,
>> for you are with me;
> your rod and your staff,
>> they comfort me.
> You prepare a table before me
>> in the presence of my enemies.
> You anoint my head with oil;
>> my cup overflows.
> Surely goodness and love will follow me
>> all the days of my life,
> and I will dwell in the house of the LORD
>> forever (Ps. 23).

41

A Celebrant in Chains

It was plain to see that the aging prisoner had suffered more than most men but there was something lively and strikingly unusual about him. Even the most cynical guards noticed that he didn't harbor any resentment or hostility towards them. The prisoner had not become hardened, even though he had been tortured and harshly treated. It was unusual for any prisoner to remain dignified, gracious, and kind, especially if he was awaiting final judgment and the verdict was likely to be execution.

Justice often moved so slowly that men literally lost their minds before their cases were decided. There was something noticeably different about this prisoner. The guards could see it shining in the depths of his eyes, in his smile, and in his confidence. Everyone wondered how he could be chained day and night without becoming embittered and despondent. Yet the prisoner was anything but despairing. Nor had he been abandoned like so many other prisoners, for he often received visitors and letters. He corresponded frequently with the outside world, and most of what he wrote had nothing to do with his personal legal troubles, or even the conditions of his imprisonment.

Several years ago the prisoner was involved in a riot in another city, which resulted in his being charged with a political offense similar to 'creating a public disturbance.' In the aftermath of the riot, he had been arrested and charged with anti-government activity. The military police beat him thoroughly and then forced him into manacles in the dark dungeon underneath the small local jail.

Eventually they released him and banished him from their jurisdiction. In spite of the terrible experience and situation he had encountered in that place he had nevertheless been able to form some close friendships, including with the officer in charge of the prison. One of those friends had recently come to visit him during his current imprisonment in the capital city. He was deeply moved by the concern of that friend at a time when almost everyone else had abandoned him. When the visit was over and his friend was preparing to return home, the prisoner gave him a letter to take back to the others.

When they received the hand-delivered letter, they were astounded at its cheer. It was unlike a letter anyone would expect from a man chained and in prison, for it contained neither personal complaints nor any trace of cynicism. The letter overflowed with joy and hope. The prisoner, despite his chains, sounded as if he was celebrating in the midst of conditions that would cause most people to chafe in anger or to become resigned and depressed. But the tone of his letter overflowed with a sense of joy. Chains and guards may have controlled his body, but his life was not shackled by the humiliation and pain of imprisonment.

I have a copy of that letter and I read it often. With each reading I am moved by the joy and hope of a prisoner who was eventually sentenced to death and executed. Even though he was probably innocent of the charges brought against him and even though he was subjected to every cruelty and humiliation of the system, his letter expresses a profound joy and hope in Jesus Christ. His expressed desire and deepest passion was to share fully in the life of Jesus Christ. Suffering and the possibility of death had not discouraged him, and his letter exudes a joyous confidence. Despite chains, torture, and the gaping uncertainty of his trial, his letter is an encouragement to me.

The prisoner was Paul and the letter was written to his friends in Philippi during his imprisonment in Rome. It is a unique letter and is frequently referred to as the epistle or letter of joy. More than any other New Testament writing, Paul's letter to his Philippian friends radiates with joy and hope. Paul's hope as a chained prisoner was a resurrection hope and he fully expected to share in the victory which Jesus had won. But in the meantime, in his ever-present suffering and chains, he accepted suffering as the honor of participating in the fellowship of Christ's own suffering. And he considered his shackles, and all of the other 'bad' things that happened to him, as having a holy purpose and meaning. God was working through his suffering to encourage the uncourageous and to inspire faith among the unbelieving. Even prison guards were touched by his witness and responded to the message of God's grace.

Nowhere does celebration take on greater meaning than in the midst of conditions that, from a human perspective, defy any reason to celebrate. It seems to me that hope and joy often develop stronger roots in the hard soil of pain and suffering than in the soft soil of comfort and plenty. Part of the malaise of our Western Christianity might well be that the soil of our lives is so rich that the root system of our faith doesn't go very deep. Around the world in the most difficult circumstances and places I encounter some of the most amazing followers of Jesus Christ who are celebrants of the cross – celebrants bound by heavy chains of poverty, oppression, calamity, and imprisonment. Some of those who suffer cannot read to study the Bible, and their theological understanding is very weak. Yet they cling passionately to hope in Jesus Christ because He alone sustains them in their suffering, and He alone is their life beyond the pain.

People like Paul and those who suffer with Christ today are truly celebrants in chains, and they put me to shame. I have so many things going for me, so much freedom, so many attractive options, and so much to live for that the real gospel seems more rooted in my head than in my heart. Sometimes I think that a little suffering would be clarifying and purifying, but I'm afraid of suffering because it hurts and I don't like to be restrained – and I wonder if my faith would stand the test with unquenchable confidence and joy in Jesus Christ.

> I thank my God every time I remember you. In all my prayers for all of you, I always pray with joy because of your partnership in the gospel from the first day until now, being confident of this, that he who began a good work in you will carry it on to completion until the day of Christ Jesus. It is right for me to feel this way about all of you, since I have you in my heart; for whether I am in chains or defending and confirming the gospel, all of you share in God's grace with me. God can testify how I long for all of you with the affection of Christ Jesus. And this is my prayer: that your love may abound more and more in knowledge and depth of insight, so that you may be able to discern what is best and may be pure and blameless until the day of Christ, filled with the fruit of righteousness that comes through Jesus Christ – to the glory and praise of God...Yes, and I will continue to rejoice, for I know... what has happened to me will turn out for my deliverance. I eagerly expect and hope that I will in no way be ashamed, but will have sufficient courage so that now as always Christ will be exalted in my body, whether by life or by death. For to me, to live is Christ and to die is gain (Phil. 1:3-11, 18-21).

42

FINDING CHRIST IN INDIA

History records that the Christian gospel came to India during the early part of the first century. Ancient churches with ancient traditions attest to the historic presence and influence of the Christian church within the context of India's majority Hindu culture. Yet, through the centuries, Christianity has continued only as a minority faith, with less than two percent of the entire population identifying itself as being Christian today. Pondering this reality during my recent travels in India, I wondered why the good news of Jesus Christ has not made more of an impact there and in other parts of the world.

During my conversations with various people as I traveled through India, I asked them about this. Repeatedly I was informed that Jesus is actually quite revered among many Hindus, particularly among many of the Brahmin people. One Brahmin observed recently that Christians in India cannot possibly be followers of Jesus since 'if they really knew Jesus they would live lives very different from the way they now live.' While his observation may have been an unfair generalization or perhaps even a critical overstatement of reality, the observation probably contained a grain of truth, since the Christian religion in India, as elsewhere, almost always obscures the living reality of Jesus. As followers of Jesus focus more on institutions and forms of religious devotion, they become increasingly alienated from Jesus – and less relevant to the lives of people within their culture.

One of the most-honored Indian leaders of modern times, Mahatma Gandhi, was greatly influenced by and attracted to Jesus. If it hadn't been for what he perceived as the outward displays of Christianity that were inconsistent with the teachings of Jesus, he said that he could have been persuaded to be a Christian. Even though the example of Jesus had a profound impact on him, Gandhi was greatly bothered by the fact that Jesus's life and teachings were not exemplified in the lives of people who claimed to be His followers. More often than not, what he observed among them reflected the modern malaise of the world, which he saw as being:

- Wealth without work,
- Pleasure without conscience,
- Science without humanity,
- Knowledge without character,
- Politics without principles,
- Commerce without morality,
- Worship without sacrifice.

Contrary to Gandhi's observations about anemic Christian practice, church history records a very dynamic beginning for the Christian faith in India. Several years after the death and resurrection of Jesus, St Thomas the disciple traveled to the southern part of India. Knowing neither the language nor the culture, St Thomas spent his time learning the language, observing the customs, and engaging with the culture of the Indian people. He observed the morning ritual of devout Hindus who made their way down to the river at the dawn of each day. Scooping water into their cupped hands, they lifted their hands up to the rising sun and prayed, 'Oh light, lead me to that light; oh truth, lead me to that truth.'

As St Thomas began to understand their prayers and learned to communicate in their language, he affirmed their prayers and told them, 'I have seen the light, and I know the truth.' The people were greatly taken aback by his bold assertion and rejected it as impossible, for, they said, 'If you had seen the light and if you know the truth, you would not be here; you would be with the gods.'

Yet St Thomas persisted in his claim to know the Light and the Truth and eventually the Hindu leaders decided to put his claim to a test. 'We will see if you are telling the truth,' they challenged him. 'Come with us to the river in the morning. Take up the water in your hands and throw it to the sky. If it stays there and doesn't fall back to the river, we will know that you have told us the truth. But if the water falls back from where it came, we will know you are a liar, and you will die.'

Oral tradition states that St Thomas went down to the river the next morning and took the water into his hands praying, 'Oh Lord, I doubted you once but I no longer doubt you. Not for my sake but for the sake of these people, that they may believe, take this water into the heavens.' Having prayed, he scooped water from the river with his hands and threw it up toward the sky – and it disappeared. From that day forward, those who were present immediately believed his witness about Jesus as the Truth and the Light. They returned to their temple, removed the images of the gods, and set them outside. Their temple became the first church in India, a meeting place for believers in Jesus. As faith in Jesus spread, the church grew and spread. The architecture of the early churches in India was similar to the architecture of the Hindu temples.

Yet during modern times the church in India has become increasingly Westernized and alienated from the Hindu culture. The gospel, which took root in the soil of India during the first century, today often seems more like a foreign religion disconnected from the culture of the people. While the person of Jesus continues to hold great attraction, the message of Jesus is often proclaimed in terms that are disconnected from the context. A witness to the Jesus of Western civilization and culture has supplanted the historic witness of St Thomas, and Christianity as religion is obscuring the reality of Jesus among His followers.

Yet there is evidence of Jesus in India. He can be seen among nuns who are providing care and shelter for disgraced and abused prostitutes; among compassionate men and women who provide homes for orphans and for the abandoned and neglected children of prisoners; and among simple, illiterate believers who simply kneel in their parched fields to pray for rain, and it rains. Jesus can also be seen in the radiant smiles of rejected and dishonored prisoners who are clinging to love and dignity in Him, their only hope for redemption and salvation. I think Jesus can also be seen in the glimmer of recognition among those who still are seeking to know the Truth and see the Light.

> 'But you will receive power when the Holy Spirit comes on you; and you will be by witnesses in Jerusalem, and in all Judea and Samaria, and to the ends of the earth.' ...They devoted themselves to the apostles' teaching and to the fellowship, to the breaking of bread and to prayer. Everyone was filled with awe, and many wonders and miraculous signs were done by the apostles. All the believers were together and had everything in common. Selling their possessions and goods, they gave to anyone as he had need. Every day they continued to meet together... They broke bread in their homes and ate together with glad and sincere hearts, praising God and enjoying the favor of all the people. And the Lord added to their number daily those who were being saved (Acts 1:8; 2:42-47).

43

COME WORSHIP THE LORD

I wish you could join me for just an hour in Upper Prison of Kampala, Uganda – in the maximum security section of prisoners condemned to death. It's virtually a prison within a prison and is called 'the condemned section' or just 'condemned.' Cut off from the rest of the prison population and surrounded by imposing stone walls the condemned prisoners have no view or access to the world outside. The men are isolated, completely confined to the dull regime of passing time – waiting, waiting, waiting – hoping against hope that they will receive a pardon or a reprieve from being executed.

I have found the condemned section one of the most thrilling places in the world to visit. What makes it so awe inspiring has little to do with condemned men clinging to shreds of hope until they receive the good news of pardon or reprieve. What makes the condemned section of Upper Prison so unusual is the joy inside: a pervasive spirit of joy among men who are worshiping the Lord of life in the face of condemnation and death. Most of the two hundred or more condemned men who are literally waiting out their lives meet together daily for praise and worship – celebrating their new life, their forgiveness, and redemption in Jesus Christ. So palpable and infectious is the joy and love of these men that it transforms the tiny concrete courtyard where they meet into a sanctuary of worship that resounds with songs of condemned men who have been set free. They are a living, vibrant, worshiping community praising the Lord in the jaws of death.

Most of the condemned prisoners have nothing. Many of them have lost all contact with their families and friends on the outside. They have no resources and sometimes not even the memory of life on the outside to sustain them. Some of the men don't even own a stitch of clothing beyond their threadbare prison-issued shorts and teeshirts. But in the midst of it all they have even started a small choir and a worship band. The songs they sing are often original compositions transcribed onto bits of paper. The band plays on instruments that have been fashioned from scraps of wood and tin, pieces of leather, twine, and makeshift drums. And when the band plays and the choir sings the sounds of worship resound beyond the walls of 'condemned' into the prison beyond. 'I have nothing left to offer you,' they sing, 'except to sing this song of praise to you, oh Lord.'

It is always difficult for me to leave my brothers in 'condemned,' for they really know how to worship the Lord. I would rather spend an hour in praise, worship, and fellowship with these men than in the finest church with the best-trained choir and the most professional musicians in the world. For as they raise their hands and hearts in worship there is an otherworldly light of joy in the eyes of the prisoners, a vibrant hope in their voices, and the presence of holy love among them that reflects God's amazing grace and glory.

I've experienced worship in other prisons just like this, including a much smaller group of life-sentenced prisoners in 'G' Hall of Stanley Prison in Hong Kong. At the time, 'G' Hall held a group of prisoners who called themselves the 'Fringe People,' comprised of men who had been convicted of capital crimes and sentenced to life imprisonment – real life. The men of the

'Fringe People' had each experienced the grace and mercy of God at a time when society had no mercy for them; they were cut off from the outside world, and would probably never see the light of day again. They began meeting daily to encourage one another and to celebrate their forgiveness, new life, and hope in Jesus Christ. Like the men in the condemned section of Upper Prison, the 'Fringe People' worshiped the Lord with such joy and vitality that it overpowered the shuddering, sinister reality of maximum security and life imprisonment. As I met with the 'Fringe People' in the hard steel and concrete world of 'G' hall, we sang together with tears of joy flowing down our faces:

> Because He lives I can face tomorrow;
>> Because He lives all fear is gone;
> Because I know He holds the future,
>> And life is worth the living just because He lives!

Oh how I wish that you and I could worship the Lord together like these condemned men.

> Come, let us sing for joy to the Lord;
>> let us shout aloud to the Rock of our salvation.
> Let us come before him with thanksgiving
>> and extol him with music and song.
> For the Lord is the great God,
>> the great King above all gods.
> In his hand are the depths of the earth,
>> and the mountain peaks belong to him.
> The sea is his, for he made it,
>> and his hands formed the dry land.
> Come, let us bow down in worship,
>> let us kneel before the Lord our Maker;
> for he is our God
>> and we are the people of his pasture,
>> the flock under his care (Ps. 95:1-7).

44

THE FEAR FACTOR

When I was much younger I was afraid of many things. I started out being afraid of the dark. I was also afraid of the thunderstorms that would sweep down from the mountains, booming their way across the exposed prairie highlands where we lived. I was afraid of the sixth-grade bully who swaggered and ruled the playground of our school. I was afraid of nuclear war with the Soviets and fallout from the atomic bombs which the Americans were testing underneath the desert south of Canada. I was afraid of dying young. I was afraid of grizzly bears. I was afraid of hellfire and damnation too.

With the passing of time I became less afraid of these things and soon only vestiges of fear remained. I enjoy the dark and thunderstorms. The bully seemed to shrink as I grew up. The possibility of nuclear war still bothers me a bit. As for grizzly bears, I met a man who taught me how to face them down – it works – and my fear of hellfire and damnation have been replaced with a sense of God's love and forgiveness.

Yet, today I am still afraid. In place of the simple fears of childhood, a plethora of more complex fears have taken root. I am afraid of failure and not measuring up to my own and other's expectations. Criticism is quite unnerving, and I am prone to cover up my mistakes and shortcomings from public view. I am afraid of being rejected or not being thought well of by people I respect. I am afraid to give too much away – information, control, and possessions. I am afraid of time passing by too quickly and of growing old and feeble and unproductive. I am afraid of being out of control and becoming dependent.

There is a great deal of fear in the world. While the things that used to make me afraid – thunder and lightening, the glare of my grammar school principal, the bully who lived down the street, asking a girl to go out on a date with me, grizzly bears and poisonous rattlesnakes – are all fears I have overcome, I find that fear is still no stranger to my life. Recently as I was flipping through the channels of the television I encountered two completely contrasting kinds of fear. First, *Fear Factor* caught my attention, a rather mind-dulling 'reality' program that pits an array of competitors against a variety of fear-inducing challenges ranging from the squeamish (eating live cockroaches) to the physically dangerous (jumping from a helicopter onto a speeding lorry to retrieve a flag, and climbing back up into the helicopter again – most flags wins!).

I don't think I'd want to do such things, and it's partly because of the fear associated with physical risk. Just moments after my encounter with *Fear Factor* I switched the television channel to the evening news and came face to face with another kind of fear – the fear of people in the shocking aftermath of a bloody suicide bombing in Iraq. I saw the real fear of people terrorized by destruction and death over which they had no control, and from which they had no escape, no safety chutes, or other options. They were trapped in danger and trauma with no way of knowing where or when the next car bomb might explode.

A few years ago the slogan 'No Fear' could be found emblazoned on teeshirts, caps, and even bumper stickers plastered on cars. It was a defiant rallying-shout born out of the physical bravado of triathlete and 'iron-man' competitions – a declaration of invincibility and fearlessness. But when our fear is born in realities and places beyond our control, beyond personal daring-do and sportive competition, such fear cannot be contained by declarations of 'no fear.' Real fear is both reasonable and irrational, a life-distorting condition over which many of us have no control at all.

There are times when I've known such fear – gut-wrenching, mind-possessing, soul-numbing fear – in the grip of circumstances and forces I hardly recognize and often can't describe. It is in times of fear that I've felt overwhelmed by a sense of captivity, of being unable to comprehend, control, conquer, or do anything to compensate against fear – completely helpless. In the grip of such fear there is no clear path of avoidance or escape and no safe and sure place of refuge.

The first mention of fear in the Bible occurs in the account of Adam losing his innocence, when he and Eve are suddenly gripped by their realization of overwhelming naked vulnerability. Even their fig-leaf camouflage proves inadequate when they hear the approaching footsteps of the Lord. Mortally afraid, Adam and Eve hide in the Garden, among the trees, desperately hoping that their fig leaves will not wilt or fall, hoping to escape discovery, embarrassment, confrontation, and its consequences.

'I was afraid because I was naked;' states Adam matter-of-factly, 'so I hid' (Gen. 3:10). His was not the explanation of the losing competitor in a *Fear Factor* clothing challenge, and it was a far cry from the 'no fear' taunt of competitive supremacy. It was the admission of deep fearfulness, about being naked, vulnerable ,and out of control. His was the kind of fear by which we as human beings kill or are killed by each other, the kind of fear that causes us to fight until we are cornered or to flee by any possible means of escape. When fight and flight both become impossible, we taste naked fear!

The reality is that the things we fear can actually take control of our lives. When we are gripped by fear of cyclones, earthquakes, or tsunamis we will inevitably keep a wary eye on signs that portend the slightest change in the sky, sea, or earth beneath us. When we fear the power of other human beings we invest inordinately in protection, looking over our shoulders and around every corner in anticipation of attack. And when we fear being vulnerable, criticized, and insulted as persons our lives will be given to masquerade and hiding. But if we fear the Lord, Scripture says it is 'the beginning of wisdom.'

We live in a world and at a time when it is practically impossible not to be afraid of something. We fear for our children and their survival in a ravaged environment. We fear for our own future and quality of life in an uncertain economy. We fear for our day-to-day safety and our familiar way of life in the face of terrorism and threats beyond our control. We are afraid, and although we may cover up or minimize our fears, we are not immune. Fig leaves are not enough to cover up our deepest fears, even though they hide our naked vulnerability. What on earth can we do? We can run but not hide; we can hide but not escape.

In the face of danger and fear David declared, 'Even though I walk through the valley of the shadow of death, I will fear no evil, for you are with me ...' (Ps. 23:4); and again, 'Though an army besiege me, my heart will not fear; though war break out against me, even then will I be confident ...'(Ps. 27:3); and, 'When I am afraid, I will trust in you. In God, whose word I praise, in God I trust; I will not be afraid. What can mortal man do to me?' (Ps. 56:3-4).

When Jesus walked upon this fear-riddled earth he responded to the common and the deepest fears of humanity again and again with the assurance of the Father's loving care and protection.

Without warning, a furious storm came up on the lake, so that the waves swept over the boat... 'Lord, save us! We're going to drown!' [the disciples cried]. He replied, 'You of little faith, why are you so afraid?' Then he got up and rebuked the winds and the waves, and it was completely calm. The men were amazed and asked, 'What kind of man is this? Even the winds and the waves obey him!' (Matt. 8:24-27).

Peace I leave with you; my peace I give you. I do not give to you as the world gives. Do not let your hearts be troubled and do not be afraid (John 14:27).

In this world you will have trouble. But take heart! I have overcome the world (John 16:33).

45

PRAYERS FROM THE BELLY OF THE WHALE

I have little difficulty praying whenever I find myself in trouble, or when I am troubled. My prayer erupts spontaneously – the natural cry of the soul confronted with pressing difficulties, imminent dangers, or stifling worries. When my situation seems totally out of my control, I see no alternative but to bend my knees and pray. As in Jonah's fearful, dark, and lonely (not to mention slimy) experience in the belly of the great fish, in desperation all I can do is to call upon the Lord in His mercy to come to my aid.

Maybe you have experienced something similar. When vicious turbulence threatens to throw the plane from the sky down to the ground, in fear and panic I cry out for God to bring us down in safety. When my wife is diagnosed with cancer, in agony I cry out for God to spare her life. When I am climbing and find myself dangerously perched on a high mountain ledge from which I can't turn back, in fear I cry to the Lord to give me strength and a way out of my predicament. When I have taken on far more responsibilities and duties than I can possibly manage and I'm committed way over my head, in desperation I turn to the Lord for wisdom and for strength. When my nephew's wife storms out on their three-month marriage, in pain I cry for the Lord to reconcile them amid the harsh words and raw emotions. When I travel in desperate lands where people are trapped in poverty, violence, and suffering and there is nothing I can do to comfort them, I pray to the Lord for mercy and for justice. From the belly of the whale I find myself crying out to God.

It takes no discipline to pray amid the churning, stifling darkness of life's desperate situations. But when life is good and normal, when things are going quite well, I find it is more difficult to pray. How do I really stay in touch with God when my needs are small? What is the place of prayer in my life when the sky is blue and the earth is firm and I'm not churning in the belly of the whale?

I came across a survey that was conducted among clergy and other Christian leaders. One of the most interesting findings of the study was that, on average, they spent less than five minutes a day in personal prayer. The problem with this is not the small amount of time but that it implies there is no sense of need for prayer, no sense of dependence on the Lord in normal circumstances. Typically when individuals or groups find themselves in precarious situations or when they are facing a crisis, prayer becomes a more significant feature of their life. But when they are content with life and feel in control of their situations, there is a tendency to turn aside from prayer and go about one's business.

On one occasion Jesus' disciples asked him to teach them to pray, and in response Jesus gave them that great model prayer which we know today as 'the Lord's Prayer.' St Matthew's account of this incident indicates that Jesus gave the disciples this model prayer and then went on to remind them of their total dependence on God. Even as the birds of the air and the flowers of the field are totally dependent on God, He told them, so is man – for neither man's endeavor to anticipate and provide for his future needs, nor his focus and preoccupation with immediate needs, overcomes the fact that he is dependent on God's providence.

The simple fact is that whether we know it or not, whether we are in crisis or ease, whether we feel comfortable or diseased, whether satisfied or needy, in the belly of the whale or on the firm dry land, we are always in a precarious state of dependence on God. Our situation is precarious in precisely the same way that both an iris growing in a field and a crocus growing in the crevice of a rock are completely at the mercy of God to nourish, sustain, and provide for them so that they can fulfill the purpose for which He created them.

In Latin, the words *prayer* and *precarious* are derived from the same root word. *Prayer* and *precarious* are related, and praying is a recognition of our precarious condition – our total dependence on the Lord who provides for us so that we too can fulfill the purpose for which He made us. Therefore we pray knowing that we are in a fragile place filled with dangers and fears, but we turn to the Lord and trust Him even to give us our daily bread and to deliver us from evils we cannot even see.

This, then, is how you should pray:
'Our Father in heaven,
hallowed be your name,
your kingdom come,
your will be done
    on earth as it is in heaven.
Give us today our daily bread.
Forgive us our debts,
    as we also have forgiven our debtors.
And lead us not into temptation,
but deliver us from the evil one' (Matt. 6:9-13).

46

EVIL FIGHTERS

Evil is generally not a pleasant topic for teatime conversation. It is unsettling, distasteful, and we'd prefer to avoid dealing with its reality. Yet the presence of evil is inescapable. Newspaper headlines proclaim the daily litany of criminal violence, scandal, terrorism, and corruption. Entertainment serves up an ever-expanding menu of sexual escapades, brutal murder, mindless mayhem, and cunning chicanery. And somehow, as if to prove that evil does not pay, we put perverts, pushers of drugs, and pickaxe murderers into prison.

Sometimes we envision evil personified, as a dark force, a spiritual ogre intent on making trouble, a sinister interference yet sometimes attractive force seducing men and women away from the light of God's goodness – away from faith in Him and consideration of their neighbor. The fact of an evil force that presents us with alternatives to what is true and good is unavoidable, for every person alive experiences personal temptations to do that which ought not to be done, and to avoid doing that which rightfully should be done. Even St Paul was painfully aware of the ongoing confrontation between right and wrong being played out in his own life. He portrayed it as a battle between good and evil being waged in his innermost being. So powerful was the conflict that in order for good to prevail St Paul needed outside help; he depended on God to resist the inclination toward evil.

This inner spiritual battle is seen by many people to be a kind of morality play in which the moral decisions of individual human beings are the spoils of battle. Right moral choices signal the victory of good over evil and Christians often focus on the spiritual battleground in terms of individual morality. The good news of Jesus Christ is proclaimed and demonstrated to individuals who are living in sin and in alienation from God. The call to repentance and faith in Jesus Christ is the good news of forgiveness for sin and evil, and the possibility of a new way of living life with God's help.

This is fantastic! This is the remedy against evil's destructive clutch in every human heart. By God's grace there is hope. Individuals can be transformed. But there is more to evil than individual morality. Evil exerts an influence that is seen not only in the human heart but also in the character of human institutions and systems. I have encountered many morally decent and upright people who hold positions of power and authority in government, industry, and various institutions and bureaucracies that are destructive and oppressive. I've often wondered why persons who are kind, conscientious, clean-living, and moral – often, even 'Christian' – are often unaware of or unwilling to confront the evil and destructive character of the systems in which they participate.

I once asked an individual to tell me how it was possible for him to quietly tolerate and accept the abuse, injustice, and inhumanity of the prison system in which he was an officer. 'It is not something over which I have control,' he responded. 'I wish it wasn't so, but what can I do? It's just the way things are.' Like other people who are in positions of responsibility he found himself powerless to change the system. The system seems to have an existence and power beyond just the people who work within it. It's as if the system has taken on a life of its own and often the impact of such an institution or system is hurtful and destructive, sometimes in subtly demeaning and debilitating bureaucratic ways. And most of the time, no one deliberately set out to make the system the way it is – no one is responsible!

I have come to believe, especially through my involvement with the huge bureaucracies of justice, corrections, and human services, that there is an institutional spirituality – a 'spirit' for good or evil that characterizes human institutions and systems. There is a prevailing spiritual climate or force at work in human institutions and systems that is influenced by, but goes beyond, the individual morality of those who lead and work within them. It's the combined spiritual ethos of values, attitudes, history, culture, interpersonal dynamics, alliances, and purposes at the heart of every institution or system that makes it a force for good or evil. It takes on a life and power of its own beyond the reach of its leaders, who often can only shrug their shoulders and dismiss it as simply *being the way things are!*

While in many cases this prevailing spirit might seem to be quite benign, there are many clear instances in which the impact and dynamics of the system or institution are an evil force with an evil impact on the lives of people. The dynamic is so powerful that even those who desire change find themselves unable to change the system. That's *the way things are.*

As followers of Jesus we need to understand, as St Paul did, that our witness for Christ is not only at the individual level, but in the broader context we are evil fighters. We fight against 'principalities and powers' – the systems, ethos, forces, world-view and *the way things are* that perpetrate evil, injustice, inhumanity, ill will, racism, sexism, classism, nationalism, tribalism, terrorism, elitism, cynicism, chauvinism, and similar. Our mission is to counter such evil at every level with the incisive truth of faith and the transforming redemptive love of Jesus Christ.

Finally, be strong in the Lord and in his mighty power. Put on the full armor of God so that you can take your stand against the devil's schemes. For our struggle is not against flesh and blood, but against the rulers, against the authorities, against the powers of this dark world and against the spiritual forces of evil in the heavenly realms. Therefore put on the full armor of God, so that when the day of evil comes, you may be able to stand your ground... (Eph. 6:10-13).

47

FIRE THAT COMES FROM HEAVEN

He was a man totally alone as he took his solitary and courageous position against overwhelming public opinion and the power of the state. Seldom had one man dared to risk such odds. It's difficult to imagine. In our democratic age, where the will of the majority rules, where politics and policy shift with changes in opinion polls, in the midst of our unending quest for cultural tolerance and social correctness, he would have been dismissed as having delusions of grandeur or being an obsessive-compulsive neurotic.

As I stood among the rocks on top of Mount Carmel, in the place where tradition holds that Elijah, the prophet, challenged King Ahab and the popular prophets of the day to a test, I wondered what it would have been like. On top of the mountain, in front of the king's court and crowds of spectators, Elijah challenged the prophets of Baal to prove their god by sending fire from Heaven to ignite the altar of their sacrifice.

For most of that day the prophets performed a frenzy of futile rites and incantations, calling upon Baal to act with fire and authority. As the sun was setting there was still no fire on the altar and all eyes turned to Elijah as he taunted the prophets and called for the altar of the Lord God Almighty to be doused with water. To the spectators it was probably comical at first, but then

Elijah called upon the Lord to act and immediately the sodden alter burst into flame.

Not a sign remains of the two altars that were built that day, or of the fire that fell from Heaven that consumed the wood and sacrifice and very rocks of the altar before which Elijah prayed. All that remains is the memory of a day when the wisdom of the majority was put to shame by the God who answered Elijah's prayer. As I stood on the hallowed ground of Mount Carmel I wondered what it would have been like to be present when the fire came. How dramatic, how unequivocal, how powerful the singular act of God in response to Elijah's simple prayer. Neither the king, nor the people, nor the popular prophets in all their finery anticipated the God who acts. To them, Elijah with his belief in the One True God was a ridiculously quaint man, out of step with modern times. There was no reason to believe that he was more than that.

On that day, however, the Lord answered Elijah and His fire consumed the altar! As I gazed down into the valley below the mountain I saw that life continues. Traffic was coursing down the highways and people were moving about their daily work. I wondered what meaning the fire that fell from Heaven has to anyone today. The world hasn't changed that much and there is probably no less need for God to prove Himself in the midst of today's world, which is also shaped and swayed by popular culture, pragmatic politics, and eclectic religion. It is not uncommon for those of us who believe in the Lord God of all creation to wish that He would show Himself somehow – that He would send a fire from Heaven that would unequivocally demonstrate that He exists and that He alone is God. Wouldn't that settle the matter once for all!

As I descended from Mount Carmel still pondering the fire of God I thought about the experiment I saw in a Taiwanese prison for repeat drug offenders. It was a very unusual situation in which one section of the prison had been given to a Christian group to run, and a similar section given to a popular cultural/

religious society. The corrections department was studying the relative impact of the two programs on inmate rehabilitation in order to determine whether the Christian way or the other way was more effective. 'It is just like the standoff between Elijah and the prophets of Baal,' I thought to myself. Which one of them will prove to be true? I think I saw a glimmer of the answer in the peace, joy, and love that inhabited the one and not the other.

At the base of Mount Carmel, I suddenly realized that what I had seen and heard in Taiwan and in countless other places and other ways is a continuing challenge. Faith in the Living God will always run counter to popular opinion and the ideologies of the day. In each generation the faith of those who believe in God is put to the test. In response to Elijah's faith and faithfulness God sent down a fire from Heaven. In response to the faith and faithfulness of believers in other generations God has shown himself in different ways. How will God show Himself in our times? I don't really know, but I think the test is probably not on a mountaintop but in the gutters and the streets where the holy fire of God's love is releasing addicts from their slavery, prisoners from the evil of their ways, and people like you and me from living meaningless and empty lives. The fire of the Lord has not burned out. The Lord continues to show himself through those who follow Him in love, joy, peace, patience, kindness, goodness, faithfulness, gentleness, and self-control, which are the fruits of the Holy Spirit – the fire of God from Heaven.

> So I say, live by the Spirit, and you will not gratify the desires of the sinful nature ... [which] are obvious: sexual immorality, impurity and debauchery; idolatry and witchcraft; hatred, discord, jealousy, fits of rage, selfish ambition, dissensions, factions and envy; drunkenness, orgies, and the like.... But the fruit of the Spirit is love, joy, peace, patience, kindness, goodness, faithfulness, gentleness and self-control... God cannot be mocked. A man reaps what he sows... Therefore, as we have opportunity, let us do good to all people...
> (Gal. 5:16, 19-23; 6:7, 10).

48

CRY JUSTICE!

At the beginning of Advent each year I hang strings of white lights from the bottom to the very top of an eight-meter spruce tree in front of my house. It is something I really look forward to, for to me those lights are no routine reflection of Christmas festivity. Instead they have become a symbol, an expression of my deepest yearning for justice, and righteousness. The cry of my heart is for the light of truth, justice and peace to break into the black night of inhumanity, inequity, and injustice.

From genocide-ravaged Rwanda to the conflictive terror in the Middle East; from Cambodia's ghastly killing fields to Auschwitz's silent silhouette of horror; from the blood-soaked ground of brutality and massacre in Africa to the suffering of the urban poor in Asia and Latin America; from crime-ravaged urban streets to the dungeons of depravity and exploitation; from the acrid stench of refugee camps to the perfumed glamour of beauty contests and fashion shows; from garbage-dump villages to consumer-bloated marketplaces; from the cowering eyes of defenseless victims to the tyrannical glare of men possessed by power – I find myself increasingly affected by the brokenness, suffering, and inequality of human life. Even those of us who are among the most privileged and protected people in the world don't have far to venture beyond our islands of security to see the terrible mess we're in. Humanity is crying out for justice and peace! So I string the lights on my Advent tree and pray for justice and peace to come!

The painful condition of the world is not very different today compared to 2000 years ago. In spite of the overlays of awesome progress in technology, medicine, and every area of human endeavour, progress alone has failed to secure justice, freedom, and peace for millions of suffering people. Like these people today the times preceding Jesus's birth were characterized by desperate yearning for justice. The advance of the Roman Empire, with all the accoutrements of civilization, its notions of civic duty, and its code of justice, served the interests of many but left countless other people oppressed and in servitude. Ever since Pompey conquered it in 63 BC, the aching cry and expectation of Israel was for the Messiah to be sent from God in order to throw off the yoke of imperialistic Roman arrogance and exploitation. Surely the Messiah would act to vanquish the oppressor and restore justice, freedom, and dignity to the suffering people of God. Hope faded over time but could not be extinguished as they waited and waited and waited for the Messiah to come.

As I put up my Advent lights I do so in solidarity and with hope and expectation that God will act, that His Kingdom of justice and peace will descend among us in this world. I meditate on Jesus, the Messiah, who finally did come. He was born amid brutality and injustice, where even babes in arms were not safe from political tyranny and megalomania. His family was a socially marginalized people in an occupied nation. Like people today who are powerless and subservient, they were subjected to the bureaucratic mandate to register their familial and racial (ethnic) identity. There was no compassionate consideration given to Mary who, although she was nine months pregnant, was also required to make the arduous journey to Bethlehem to register in the place where she belonged. Notwithstanding labor pains and the imminence of childbirth, no hospitality was extended to her by the management or residents of the inn or even by local householders. Crowded out, rootless in their own familial home town, and without any other means, they took refuge in an unsanitary cattle shed. And so Jesus, the Messiah, was born in a barn. I light my Advent tree for Jesus, who came in solidarity with the poor of the world.

Jesus' birth in such conditions was just the beginning. His birth was immediately overshadowed by a monstrous act of genocide perpetrated by a fearful king (Herod) who thought that his power was being threatened by an infant. To ensure his hold on power, he had every baby boy executed in cold blood. Jesus' family fled for safety, taking their precious infant to a foreign land. Now they were not only homeless but also stateless refugees, second-class residents on foreign soil. Egypt had never been a hospitable place for Jewish refugees. Yet the Messiah was not broken by inhumanity and atrocity, and the hope for deliverance of the oppressed could not be extinguished.

When evening shadows fall at the end of the day, I light my tree and take heart in its simple glow, which shines against the night. Advent is a time of anticipation and expectation. It is a time of longing and hope. Jesus the Messiah has come. Justice and peace will yet triumph. This is good news for all of us who cry for justice. We cry justice for the abandoned children of prisoners in Nepal and Madagascar. We cry justice for the oppressed and persecuted Christians in Sudan, and for young Maoris, Aboriginals, Indigenous Indians, and Gypsies who face discrimination. We cry justice for those in Rwanda and Burundi living with the painful legacy of torture, rape, and genocide. We cry justice for those helpless children in Thailand, India, Philippines, and Brazil who are forced to prostitute themselves. We cry justice for laborers in China whose labor is exploited by the rich and the powerful. We cry justice for women abused and exploited by their own husbands. We cry justice for ourselves whenever we are misunderstood, mistreated, and misplaced.

I light my Advent tree as I cry for justice and as I yearn for Christ to set things right. Come Lord Jesus, come.

O come, O come, Emmanuel, and ransom captive Israel,
  That mourns in lonely exile here; until the Son of God appears.
O come, thou Rod of Jesse's stem, from every foe deliver them
  That trust thy mighty power to save, and give them victory o'er the grave.
O come, thou Key of David, come, and open wide our heavenly home;
  Make safe the way that leads on high, and close the path to misery.
O come, thou Day-spring from on high, and cheer us by thy drawing nigh;
  Disperse the gloomy clouds of night, and death's dark shadow put to flight.
O come, Desire of nations, bind in one the hearts of all mankind;
  Bid thou our sad divisions cease, and be thyself our King of Peace.

(From Latin plainsong, circa ninth century)

49

MESSIAHS DON'T SUFFER

I really wish God would do something about injustice in the world – now! Life is incredibly unfair for many people – not merely unfair, but essentially unjust. Yet throughout the Scriptures, it is evident that God cares intensely for the oppressed, the brutalized, and the neglected. In the face of the injustice and oppression, which afflicts so many people in different parts of the world, I wish that God would simply act to release the 'suffering innocents' from the cruelty and evil perpetrated by heartless people and systems.

The daily litany of news reports only multiplies the tremendous tension we feel between the pain of the oppressed and an Almighty God who does not seem to act. How much easier our lives as believers would be if we could count on God to straighten out the mess in the Middle East, or strike down economic opportunists who exploit cheap labor, or punish those who take advantage of innocent children to gratify their base desires.

There has always been a central tension between injustice and a righteous God who does not seem to act. With the coming of Jesus, the Messiah, people expected God to bring political liberation to His people who had been suffering under Roman occupation. While Jesus went about healing the sick, He seemed oblivious to the core injustice that was their political reality. Surely, God would act against the embarrassment of His chosen people living under subjection to pagan Gentiles.

Even Jesus' own disciples could not understand why He did not act decisively as the deliverer of God's people. In addition, when Jesus told them that He was going to suffer and die, Peter vehemently protested the Messiah's 'negative' thinking. 'Oh no, that can never happen to you,' as if to say, 'Don't be ridiculous, Messiahs don't suffer!'

Our human desperation and desire for vindication causes us to look for a strong deliverer, a Messiah who will rise above the misery and the fray, a Messiah who will not succumb to suffering but will overthrow those who cause it. It is our nature to look for leaders to lead us out of suffering, not into suffering. However, when God entered the world in the person of Jesus of Nazareth He did not do what people hoped for. He did not overrule the politics of the day; instead he offered forgiveness and peace to both rulers and those ruled. He did not vanquish the oppressors but showed them that God was among the oppressed – compassionate, merciful, wounded, and sharing their suffering.

In the upside-down Kingdom of God, the politics of men who would use power to change the world gives way to a savior who overcomes evil and death by taking upon himself the suffering and injustice of the whole world. To follow Jesus, the Messiah, is to follow Him into the affliction of the world. God came to set things right, not by turning the tables of power, or by avenging evil-doers. Rather he came as a loving Heavenly Father to shoulder our sorrows, to carry our burdens, to forgive us our sins, and to heal our injustices. Our Messiah suffers, He takes our wounds upon Himself, and He is with us in the crucible of our agony and need.

It would easier to believe in a God who shows Himself as an avenger who can be counted on to act. Instead, He is the compassionate Savior who shared our human suffering as one of us, absorbing our pain and healing our wounds. Yet Peter's vehement reaction to Jesus is easy for me to understand – for in the face of the injustice, oppression, and inequality of the world it would be easier to enlist in the army of a conquering Messiah than to follow the Messiah, the Suffering Servant, our Savior, into the messiness and pain of the world.

> He was despised and rejected by men,
>> a man of sorrows, and familiar with suffering.
> Like one from whom men hide their faces
>> he was despised, and we esteemed him not.
> Surely he took up our infirmities
>> and carried our sorrows,
> yet we considered him stricken by God,
>> smitten by him, and afflicted.
> But he was pierced for our transgressions,
>> he was crushed for our iniquities;
> the punishment that brought us peace was upon him,
>> and by his wounds we are healed (Isa. 53:3-5).

50

The Blessed Scandal

The small Canadian town in which I grew up was divided in two by a railroad line that ran through it. The south side of town was the more affluent part, while the north side consisted of fewer houses that were mostly smaller and poorer. There were no paved streets and the houses were not connected to the community water and sewer system. It was naturally considered the less desirable side of town and the people who lived there were commonly referred to as 'north siders' or as being from the 'other side of the tracks.' There was a stigma attached to being from the north side of town.

In prison I meet many men and women who were born on the 'wrong side' of their own town, on the 'other side of the tracks.' Often they have become stigmatized by the lack of family pedigree and their unfortunate place of origin. Frequently such prisoners blame their life-situation on their 'bad' family and genetic inheritance – the 'bad blood' of their ancestors and being born of illegitimate or questionable parentage. Sometimes they lay the blame for their behavior on the fact that they grew up on the wrong side of the tracks, and that they were raised on the seamy side of town where people are poor and family bloodlines are checkered with shady characters and whispered secrets. Thus, disposed by historical destiny, they accept their station in life and their 'bad luck' as inevitable.

I feel a measure of pity for these people because I remember some of the kids I grew up with who were also born and raised on the 'other side of the tracks.' Although some of them became my friends, those of us from the 'good' side of town tended to look down on them, mistakenly thinking ourselves as being decent and better. I am sure that our family situations made a huge difference in how we felt about ourselves and how we viewed others. There were those among us who could trace their unblemished 'blue blood' lineage down through the centuries, and with that came a sense of privilege, pride, and birthright by which they perpetuated the heritage of their family name.

By contrast, some of the less fortunate people in the world who have grown up on the 'other side' of town inherit the fruit of a misshapen, twisted family tree from which they derive little more than a heritage of indignity and a tainted sense of personal worth.

However, for most of us, tracing our family history inevitably reveals a mixture of the good, the bad, and the ugly – a mixed legacy of embarrassing family scandals and occasional shining stars hidden among generations of ordinary people. Our bloodlines are not as pure as we would prefer, and it is unsettling to realize the extent to which the fallenness of human nature erupts within our own family stories even though we may have escaped living on 'the other side of the tracks' by sheer historical accident.

In spite of his royal bloodline, Jesus of Nazareth was born on the 'other side of the tracks.' His birth to an unwed mother in a small rural town was a scandal. By all the rights on one side of His family, Jesus should have been born in the palace of the king, but He wasn't. He was not even born in the capital city. Yet His birth on the 'wrong side' became the holy scandal, for the 'pedigree' of the Savior of humankind was simultaneously holy and scandalous, Son of God and Son of Man, Holy God becoming mortal man on the wrong side of town.

By being born into human history, the Gospels portray Jesus as descending from a family lineage with its share of questionable characters, full of scandal. Consider that His family tree comprised of the likes of Tamar, the widowed daughter-in-law of Judah (Joseph's brother) who pretended to be a prostitute in order to seduce her father-in-law. Consider Rahab, the Jericho prostitute who helped the Israelites. She became the mother of Boaz. Then there was also Bathsheba, the woman who became the object of King David's illicit desire that led him to adultery, and inevitably, murder. She became the mother of Solomon. This is just a touch of the scandal that tainted the direct lineage of Jesus. Moreover, as if to cap it off, Mary the mother of Jesus became pregnant out of marriage. Scandalous indeed!

The profound hope in Jesus' scandalous birth, however, is that He was not just another person born on the right side of the tracks with an unblemished 'blue blood' family heritage. He wasn't born and raised in prosperity and privilege, looking down on 'north siders' living across the tracks. The fact that Jesus came from an impure lineage, reflecting all of the good, the bad, and the ugly aspects of human existence, makes His birth and life relevant to all people – on both sides of the track.

Do not be afraid. I bring you good news of great joy that will be for all the people. Today in the town of David a Savior has been born to you; he is Christ the Lord. This will be a sign to you: You will find a baby wrapped in cloths and lying in a manger (Luke 2:10-12).

51

SINGING WITH THE ANGELS

Music is a universal language giving expression to experiences and realities that cannot be described or contained by words alone. It is a language springing out of the depths of heart and soul.

More than any other celebration, Jesus's birth is uniquely celebrated in music. Every Christmas I find my soul uplifted as the music of the season washes over me and within me. I have often wondered why the music of this season is so special – why is it that the birth of Jesus has occasioned some of the greatest music ever written? From profound and simple carols like 'Silent Night' and 'Joy to the World' through rousing masterpieces like Handel's *Messiah* and Bach's *Christmas Oratorio*, the celebration of Jesus's birth resounds with a celebratory joy that lifts the human heart.

Why do people who seldom sing during the first eleven months of the year suddenly join in the Christmas music? Why did the angels 2000 years ago sing when they announced Jesus's birth to shepherds in the fields? It seems so incongruous that the singing of angels would herald the birth of the baby Jesus as being good news and bringing peace to all people, a baby born under extraordinarily humble circumstances, in a most inauspicious place, to very unlikely parents. Why do angels sing?

The only other biblical reference to angels singing occurs in the apocalyptic vision of St John, where the hosts of Heaven erupt in a new song of praise and worship to this same Jesus, the Savior, who was and is the 'Lamb, who was slain, to receive power and wealth and wisdom and strength and honor and glory and praise!' (Rev. 5:12). Perhaps the angels singing to announce Jesus's birth as Savior of the world was just the beginning of a song of inexpressible joy that resounds throughout the ages – an unbounded hymn of praise and worship that reaches its perfect climax in Jesus's cosmic victory over evil and death.

Why do the angels sing? I think they sing at Christmas because a Savior is born to redeem the world from sin. Angels sing because God is acting to bring hope and healing to the broken world. Angels sing because justice and peace is something to celebrate. Angels sing because Jesus has come to save the world. Angels will continue singing in triumphant praise and worship with all the company of Heaven when His victory is complete. I join the angels in their song because Jesus Christ our Savior is the King of Kings and the Lord of Lords who was, who is, and who is to come.

I think the singing of angels when Christ was born was the beginning of a song – a triumphant song of joy and praise resounding in the heavens whenever we follow Jesus by loving our neighbors, welcoming strangers, helping the weak, giving to the needy, visiting the imprisoned, and proclaiming the freedom and joy of salvation in Jesus Christ.

Now, that is making music!

Suddenly a great company of the heavenly host appeared
with the angel, praising God and saying,
    'Glory to God in the highest,
        and on earth peace to men on whom
            his favor rests' (Luke 2:13, 14).

52

GLORIA DEUS!

Long waves crested majestically, slowly, glistening in the soft rays of morning light. Enervated by the sight and sound of pungent solitude, I ran along the deserted beach scarcely cognizant of where I was. I became so mesmerized by the splendor of the morning that I found myself no longer running, but standing on the fringe between land and sea staring into the most beautiful sunrise I had ever seen. I felt suspended between earth and Heaven, filled with a sense of holy presence and a joy that could not be contained.

'Praise the Lord!' I shouted involuntarily. 'Praise my soul the King of Heaven!' I sang, flinging my face and arms skyward. Suddenly self-conscious that there might be somebody around to observe my outburst, I dropped my arms and glanced behind me and all around. Nevertheless, I was quite alone, except for the palpable presence of Heaven, the Creator's presence, gracing my solitude with the beauty of a morning masterpiece. Praise the Lord!

Morning gave way to day and the sense of joy and songs of praise would not leave my mind. There was beauty all around me – seen and unseen. I felt my earthbound soul soaring with unspeakable delight, set free from worrisome and mundane preoccupations. I stopped again to contemplate the golden sand of the seashore that stretched for miles beyond me. I could not begin to imagine the measure of God's love, which is said to be more incomprehensible than the vastness of the grains of sand on the beach. I stooped to scoop up a handful, only to realize that the number of grains in my palm were more than I had time to count. Awesome! I praised the Lord for giving me the vast sand of the beach by which to know the enormity of His love and grace!

As I looked back out to the horizon where sea and sky merge, it struck me that somewhere in the unfathomable depths of the vast ocean my failures and my faults lie buried by God's mercy. It is so hard for me to imagine that God chooses to forget that which I so painfully remember ... and remember. I praised the Lord for His gift of the sea by which I know the depth of His mercy and forgiveness.

The sun had climbed higher into the sky by the time I turned around and retraced my steps along the beach. The cool damp of early morning mist was rising from the salt marsh. Sandpipers and plovers skittered along the edge of the surf, barely beyond the water's reach. They danced and twittered in delight of morning providence, where God was giving them food from the storehouse of His sea. I praised the Lord for His gifts of sun and sand as well as fruits of land and sea by which I, too, am fed this day.

Praise the Lord!

Most High, omnipotent, good Lord
    To you belong praise and glory, honor and blessing
    No one is worthy to breathe your name.
Be praised, my Lord, for all your creatures.
In the first place for blessed Brother Sun,
    Who gives us the day and enlightens us through you.
He is beautiful and radiant with his great splendor,
    giving witness to you. Most Omnipotent One.

Be praised, my Lord, for Sister Moon and the stars
    formed by You so bright, precious and beautiful.
Be praised, my Lord, for Brother Wind
    and the airy skies, so cloudy and serene;
    for every weather, be praised, for it is life-giving.
Be praised, my Lord, for Sister Water,
    so necessary yet so humble, precious and so chaste.
Be praised, my Lord, for Brother Fire,
    He is beautiful and carefree, robust and fierce.
Be praised, my Lord, for our sister, Mother Earth,
    who nourishes us and watches us
    while bringing forth abundance of fruits
    with colored flowers and herbs.
Be praised, my Lord, for those who pardon through your love
    and bear weakness and trial.
Blessed are those who endure in peace,
    for they will be crowned by You, Most High.
Be praised, my Lord, for our sister, Bodily Death,
    whom no living man can escape.
Woe to those who die in sin.
Blessed are those who discover Your Holy Will.
The second death will do them no harm.
Praise and bless my Lord.
Render thanks, serve Him with great humility.
Amen.

                    (A prayer attributed to St Francis of Assisi)

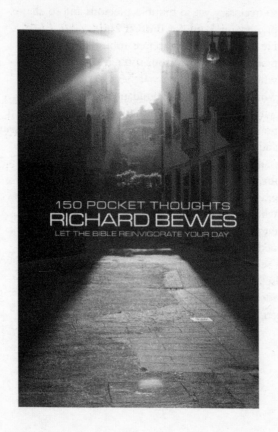

150 POCKET THOUGHTS
RICHARD BEWES
LET THE BIBLE REINVIGORATE YOUR DAY

150 Pocket Thoughts

Let the Bible reinvigorate your Day

Richard Bewes

Richard Bewes has been a pastor for over many years. He has been called on to minister to people at the heights of their joy and the depths of their despair. In all situations he has been guided by a lively faith in the God whom he serves.

From this accumulated wisdom come thoughts that will encourage you in your daily life. Whether used as a daily devotion, or for answers to specific events using the subject index, you will find a transcendency that increases your understanding of the God of creation, and your relationship to him.

Richard Bewes was until his retirement in 2005 the Rector of All Souls church in London, an accomplished broadcaster he is also a best-selling author and popular conference speaker. However he would still have liked to have added 'Wimbledon champion' to that list.

ISBN 1-85792-991-8

IN GREEN PASTURES

Devotional Readings For Every Day Of The Year

J.R. MILLER

In Green Pastures

Devotional Readings for Every Day of the Year

J R Miller

J R Miller (1840-1912), considered by many the most popular and gifted devotional writer of his era, leads us through our daily meditations, displaying his amazing gift for drawing and expounding on Gods word.

Simple, accessible and tender this is a wonderful devotional book that will enhance your quiet time, and serve as valuable source of inspiration and guidance. Miller offers a wealth of practical wisdom for our everyday lives, challenging us to seek to follow Christ's example every day of the year.

In an increasingly hectic world this is a book of immeasurable value, aiding us in taking time out, and coming into the presence of the Lord. For you this could be a timeless companion book. It is written in a beautiful and heart-warming style with a message that offers a freshness and clarity for the 21st century.

ISBN 1-84550-032-6

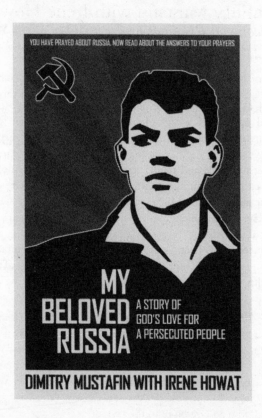

My Beloved Russia

Dimitry Mustafin's story of God's love
for a persecuted people

Dimitry Mustafin with Irene Howat

You have prayed about Russia, now read about the answers to your prayers

Dimitry Mustafin, a Professor of Inorganic Chemistry in Moscow, was given permission by the Soviet Government to work for a year in Italy – although his wife and daughter were not allowed to go in case they all defected.

Dimitry became a Christian in Milan. When he told his mother of his conversion, he learned for the first time that his grandfather had been martyred for his faith. Defection was far from his mind, instead he longed to take the gospel to his Motherland. He left Russia a Lieutenant in the Russian Chemical Army and returned… a Bible Smuggler!

Since then, Dimitry has spent his time distributing Bibles in Moscow and other parts of Russia – and sharing his faith in every way possible. As soon as Communism fell, he was in Red Square, preaching. Gideons International heard of what he and others in his congregation were doing, and they now supply Scriptures, not secretly, one at a time, but by the lorry-load.

Because of his family history, Dimitry has a deep concern for prisoners and orphan children, who also often end up in prison. He visited one of the largest prisons so often that the governor invited him to staff meetings! It was at one of these that he was introduced to a retired executioner … who worked in the prisons at the time that his grandfather was killed. Such encounters do not make for easy evangelism, yet Dimitry was able to pray with him and lead him to the saviour.

Dimitry tells his story with heart-rending honesty. You will never forget it.

Dimitry Mustafin is head of the Gideon's Moscow branch. Irene Howat is an award-winning and best-selling biographer from Scotland.

ISBN 1-84550-062-8

TO THE XTREME

THE EDDIE MURISON STORY
ANNE SUTHERLAND
& EDDIE MURISON

To the Extreme

The Eddie Murison Biography

Anne Sutherland & Eddie Murison

Eddie's criminal career began at nine years old. Between the ages of fourteen and twenty-nine he spent eleven years behind bars with convictions for assault, theft and robbery. The phrase 'miss-spent youth' doesn't do Eddie justice.

The final straw came during one prison term when an officer waited until Christmas Day to read him a letter from his wife, a letter telling him she was leaving him. Feeling as though he had nothing left in life Eddie reacted in the only way he knew how - violently.

Not long after Eddie received a visit from a Christian minister. His message of new beginnings and forgiveness for past sins awoke something in him. Eddie realised that his old life was going nowhere, he needed a new direction so he trusted and believed the good news of Jesus Christ.

From that moment on his life has never been the same. The change in Eddie's life has been so profound as to challenge the cynics who scoff at 'jailhouse conversions'.

When Eddie left prison he went on to reach out to others through a ministry to the homeless, a testimony to the power of God to renew the whole person. This inspiring biography reminds us all that whatever our situation in life, we have a God who welcomes home the prodigal.

Eddie Murison's story is one that shows that no matter how far a man goes down into the mire of sin, addiction and depravity the Lord can begin a work in that life.

Canon Noel Proctor, Former Prison Chaplain

...This book gives hope and could change lives.

Paul Cowley, Director, Alpha for Prisons

Today Eddie is Pastor of the Community Cell Church in the Mastrick area of Aberdeen. His work involves discipleship training and helping families through counselling.

ISBN 1-84550-078-4

INSPIRATIONAL GOLD
Thought-provoking meditations
from Great Christian authors

Amy Car...

John Bunyan

Francis of Assisi

...aham Kuyper

C.H. Spurge...

Francis Bacon

Cyril of Jerusalem

John We...

...th Browning

F. B. Meyer

Mary Peters

edited by
Mary Werner

Inspirational Gold

Thought-provoking meditations from Great Christian authors

Mary Werner

Do you want a daily devotional book that delivers riches every day? Fed up with meditations that barely scratch beneath the surface of your experience and understanding? Want to read something profound, something life-changing?

Mary Werner has produced a delightful daily devotional made up of quotations selected from the last twenty centuries of Christian experience. These allow us, as 21st century readers, to benefit from the wealth of wisdom of past pilgrims on the road to enlightenment.

Each day opens with a passage of the Bible that is then illuminated from the writings of Great Christian figures and authors. These gems come from a wide variety of sources, early Christians like Cyprian and Iranaeus; then Jerome, Anselm or Francis of Assissi; Thomas a Kempis; Martin Luther and Jonathan Edwards pop up; as do John Donne; Blaise Pascal and John Wesley; also included are more contemporary figures such as Frances Ridley Havergal, Harriet Beecher Stowe, George Macdonald - and many, many more from each and every century of thought.

Refined by the passage of time, these ideas remain as relevant and life-changing today as when they were written. They will enrich your times of meditation with a freshness and clarity that sets you up for the day.

Whether you use it for a few moments before the daily rush gets under way, on the train or bus, or as you wind down at night, 'Inspirational Gold' will provide the ideal companion.

ISBN 1-84550-060-1

Christian Focus Publications
publishes books for all ages

Our mission statement –

STAYING FAITHFUL

In dependence upon God we seek to help make His infallible Word, the Bible, relevant. Our aim is to ensure that the Lord Jesus Christ is presented as the only hope to obtain forgiveness of sin, live a useful life and look forward to heaven with Him.

REACHING OUT

Christ's last command requires us to reach out to our world with His gospel. We seek to help fulfill that by publishing books that point people towards Jesus and help them develop a Christ-like maturity. We aim to equip all levels of readers for life, work, ministry and mission.

Books in our adult range are published in three imprints.

Christian Focus contains popular works including biographies, commentaries, basic doctrine and Christian living. Our children's books are also published in this imprint.

Mentor focuses on books written at a level suitable for Bible College and seminary students, pastors, and other serious readers. The imprint includes commentaries, doctrinal studies, examination of current issues and church history.

Christian Heritage contains classic writings from the past.

Christian Focus Publications, Ltd
Geanies House, Fearn,
Ross-shire, IV20 1TW, Scotland, United Kingdom
info@christianfocus.com
www.christianfocus.com